Arduino and LEGO Projects

Jon Lazar

Apress·

Arduino and LEGO Projects

ISBN-13 (pbk): 978-1-4302-4929-0

ISBN-13 (electronic): 978-1-4302-4930-6

President and Publisher: Paul Manning
Lead Editor: Michelle Lowman
Developmental Editor: James Markham
Technical Reviewer: Brian Evans
Editorial Board: Steve Anglin, Mark Beckner, Ewan Buckingham, Gary Cornell, Louise Corrigan, Morgan Ertel, Jonathan Gennick, Jonathan Hassell, Robert Hutchinson, Michelle Lowman, James Markham, Matthew Moodie, Jeff Olson, Jeffrey Pepper, Douglas Pundick, Ben Renow-Clarke, Dominic Shakeshaft, Gwenan Spearing, Matt Wade, Tom Welsh
Coordinating Editor: Katie Sullivan
Copy Editor: Mary Behr
Compositor: SPi Global
Indexer: SPi Global
Artist: SPi Global
Cover Designer: Anna Ishchenko

Distributed to the book trade worldwide by Springer Science+Business Media New York, 233 Spring Street, 6th Floor, New York, NY 10013. Phone 1-800-SPRINGER, fax (201) 348-4505, e-mail orders-ny@springer-sbm.com, or visit www.springeronline.com. Apress Media, LLC is a California LLC and the sole member (owner) is Springer Science + Business Media Finance Inc (SSBM Finance Inc). SSBM Finance Inc is a Delaware corporation.

For information on translations, please e-mail rights@apress.com, or visit www.apress.com.

Apress and friends of ED books may be purchased in bulk for academic, corporate, or promotional use. eBook versions and licenses are also available for most titles. For more information, reference our Special Bulk Sales-eBook Licensing web page at www.apress.com/bulk-sales.

Any source code or other supplementary materials referenced by the author in this text is available to readers at www.apress.com. For detailed information about how to locate your book's source code, go to www.apress.com/source-code/.

To all those who pick up two bricks and snap them together.

Contents at a Glance

Contents

About the Author

Jon Lazar is a freelance developer and LEGO builder with 15+ years of experience in the technology field. He started his career at AT&T and has since helped a number of startups in the NYC area in building their digital presences and their digital infrastructures. In his free time, he is an accomplished builder of LEGO sculptures. He regularly writes about LEGO, social media, technology, and other related topics on justjon.net and can be found on Twitter at @JustJon.

About the Technical Reviewer

Brian Evans is an artist working in electronic media and Assistant Professor of Art at Metropolitan State University of Denver, where he teaches multidisciplinary courses in art on topics that include electronics and digital fabrication. He is the author of *Beginning Arduino Programming* (Apress, 2011) and *Practical 3D Printers* (Apress, 2012). He received an MFA from California State University, Long Beach in 2008, and a BFA from Arizona State University in 2005.

Acknowledgments

Jon would like to thank Mike and Lee for helping him come out of his LEGO "dark ages" and become the AFOL LEGO builder he is today. Thanks to Marwan for his assistance with the Arduino controller for the LEGO Power Functions train. And thanks to Brian for looking at the code for the projects and cleaning up and improving it.

A special thank you to the British Broadcasting Company for the permission to include the TARDIS in this book and for 50 years of Doctor Who.

Introduction

For 80 years, The LEGO Group has produced building toys for children to enjoy. As technology has advanced, they have introduced some interactive components that were limited in different ways.

The Arduino is an open source microcontroller that allows interaction with all different forms of electronic devices and sensors. It allows for many creative projects that can be controlled by a device that is a small, low-powered computer.

By combining these two flexible systems, myriad projects can be built that can do almost anything—the only limit is your imagination.

CHAPTER 1

■ ■ ■

LEGO, Arduino, and The Ultimate Machine

For years LEGO has produced their own computer based system known as Mindstorms. It gave a computer brain to the plastic LEGO bricks that had been around for decades. While Mindstorms has advanced in the 15 years since it was introduced, it was still limited based on the size of the LEGO Intelligent Brick and the available sensors and motors. An alternative to using the LEGO Mindstorms is the Arduino microprocessor, a small computer that can make use of any electrical components with some programming.

Introducing the Arduino

An Arduino (as seen in Figure 1-1) is an open source microcontroller that allows for programming and interaction; it is programmed in C/C++ with an Arduino library to allow it to access the hardware. This allows for more flexible programmability and the ability to use any electronics that can interface with the Arduino. Because the Arduino is open source, the plans for the circuits are available online for free to anyone who wants to use and create their own based on the schematics, as long as they share what they create. This allows for a lot of customizability in projects, since people have built Arduinos of different sizes, shapes, and power levels to control their projects.

Figure 1-1. *The Arduino microcontroller*

The main advantages of using the Arduino over LEGO's own motor systems are the open source base, the expandability, and the sizes. With LEGO's system, the user is locked into the pieces LEGO created. This can be a hindrance with smaller projects where the Mindstorms NXT Intelligent Brick can be too large to easily incorporate or hide the intelligence behind the project. With the smaller Arduino circuit board, less clearance is required to hold the circuit board, which means more flexibility in the design of the project. A comparison of the Arduino and the LEGO NXT brick can be seen in Figure 1-2.

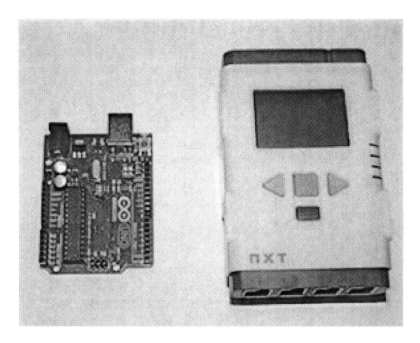

Figure 1-2. *The Arduino and the LEGO Mindstorms NXT Intelligent Brick*

The Arduino itself may not be capable of fulfilling all the activities that you would like to carry out with it, but there are circuit boards known as shields that snap on top of the Arduino circuit board to expand the usability of the Arduino. Allowing the use of motors, adding Internet connectivity, making sounds with .wav files, and other activities can be triggered through the use of these add-on boards, thus allowing the Arduino to be programmed to carry out tasks it could not without them. As an example, Figure 1-3 shows an Ethernet shield that allows the Arduino to connect to the Internet.

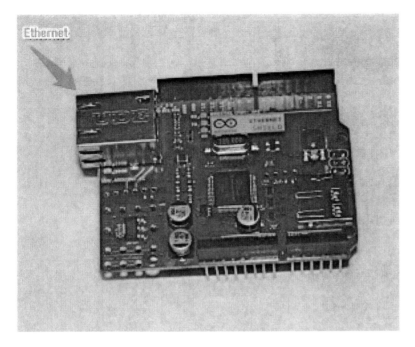

Figure 1-3. An Ethernet shield to allow the Arduino to talk to the Internet

Your First Arduino Program

Most commonly, when someone tries out a new computer language, they make the words "Hello World" appear on the screen. The Arduino version of this is to make a light-emitting diode (LED) blink. By plugging the LED into two of the ports on the Arduino and writing a simple program, the Arduino can turn the light on and off.

The first step is to put the LED into the Arduino. LEDs are specific to the way they are used. The LED needs to be plugged in so that the longer end goes into a numbered pin and the shorter pin into the ground pin, or the LED will not light up. Figure 1-4 shows the longer side in the socket labeled 13 and the shorter side in the ground.

Figure 1-4. *The LED plugged into the Ardunio*

Once the LED is firmly placed in the Arduino, the next step is to connect it to a computer via USB cable. The computer must have the Arduino software installed in order to program the Arduino. The software can be downloaded for free at arduino.cc in the download section for your computer operating system of choice. Once it is downloaded and installed, open the Arduino software. The following program can be found in File ➤ Examples ➤ 01.Basics ➤ Blink or it can be entered by hand, as shown in Listing 1-1.

Listing 1-1. Basic Blink Program

```
/*
  Blink
  Turns on an LED on for one second, then off for one second, repeatedly.

  This example code is in the public domain.
 */

// Pin 13 has an LED connected on most Arduino boards.
// give it a name:
int led = 13;

// the setup routine runs once when you press reset:
void setup() {
  // initialize the digital pin as an output.
  pinMode(led, OUTPUT);
}
```

```
// the loop routine runs over and over again forever:
void loop() {
  digitalWrite(led, HIGH);    // turn the LED on (HIGH is the voltage level)
  delay(1000);                // wait for a second
  digitalWrite(led, LOW);     // turn the LED off by making the voltage LOW
  delay(1000);                // wait for a second
}
```

The code in Listing 1-1 is the most basic program for an Arduino. It is read by the Arduino from the top down. The first thing in the program is a global variable definition for the pin that has the LED. A global variable is defined outside the setup() and loop() functions and can be accessed from anywhere in the program. The line int led=13; defines the global variable named led to be an integer with the value of 13. Whenever the word led is used, the program will interpret it as the number 13. Since the variable is defined before the words void setup(); it is what is referred to as a global variable, which means any part of the program can access and make changes to it. If the variable had been defined in the setup or loop sections (as defined below), it would only be a local variable that could only be accessed by that section of code. It is worth noting that anything between the symbols /* and */ or on a line after // are comments and will be ignored by the computer when it reads the program.

```
// the setup routine runs once when you press reset:
void setup() {
  // initialize the digital pin as an output.
  pinMode(led, OUTPUT);
}
```

Anything between the braces after setup() will be executed when the program first runs. Anything in there will be run only once and never be looked at again. In this case, it using pinMode to tell the Arduino that it will be using pin 13, where you defined led, to be used to send a signal out. It is notable that the pins can be used for either input or output, but must be defined to do so.

```
// the loop routine runs over and over again forever:
void loop() {
  digitalWrite(led, HIGH);    // turn the LED on (HIGH is the voltage level)
  delay(1000);                // wait for a second
  digitalWrite(led, LOW);     // turn the LED off by making the voltage LOW
  delay(1000);                // wait for a second
}
```

Once the setup runs, it then executes whatever is between the braces after loop(). The difference is that once the section in the loop() starts, it will start that code over again once it reaches the end. Pin 13 on the Arduino has only two states, off and on. The digitalWrite function tells the light to turn on and off based on whether it is told to be HIGH or LOW. Putting a delay between the digitalWrite statements provides the ability to see the light turn on and off rather than just a strobe effect. The delay statement will wait as long as the number in the parentheses is, in thousandths of a second.

With the code written, it needs to be uploaded to the Arduino. By connecting it with a standard USB cable, the computer can talk to the Arduino. Clicking the arrow in the upper right hand corner will compile the code and upload it to the Arduino. Once installed, it will begin to execute after several seconds and the LED will begin to blink on and off.

Programming the Ultimate Machine

The Ultimate Machine, also known as The Useless Machine, is considered the most efficient machine ever made. Its only task is to turn itself off when it is turned on. The original Ultimate Machine was created by Claude Shannon when he was working at Bell Labs in 1952. The following sections explain the steps involved.

Assembling the Arduino and Motor

In order to build the Useless Machine, a motor is required. To drive the motor, a motor shield will need to be placed on top of the Arduino. While there are a few different shields that would allow for a motor to connect to the Arduino, we will be using the Adafruit Industries motor shield because we can use it to drive the different kinds of motors you will be using in different projects in this book. Figure 1-5 shows the motor shield from Adafruit Industries in its unassembled form.

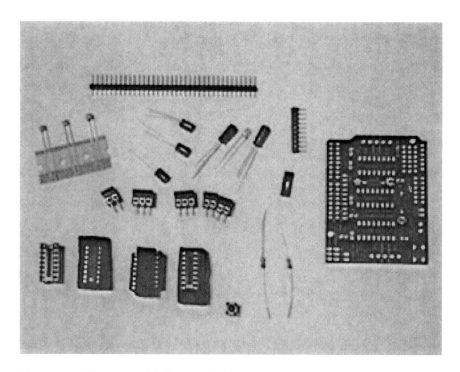

Figure 1-5. *The unassembled motor shield*

There is often considered a do-it-yourself (DIY) aspect to open source hardware, and sometimes manufactures will sell products like shields with some assembly required. With some basic soldering knowledge, they are not too complex to put together. The instructions on how to assemble it can be found at www.ladyada.net/make/mshield/solder.html. Figure 1-6 shows the motor shield assembled.

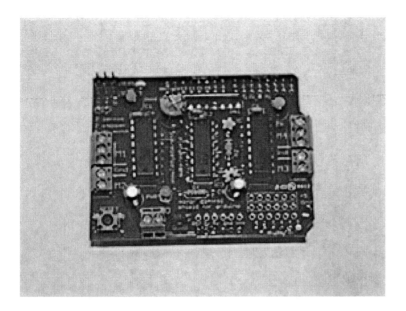

Figure 1-6. *The assembled motor shield*

Once the motor shield is soldered together, it snaps in easily on top of the Arduino. Press them together firmly but do not push too hard. Once they are together, it's time to add the motor. The Adafruit motor shield supports DC motors, servo motors, and stepper motors. For this project, you'll be using a servo motor. The motor's wires plug in on the top left on the three pronged plugs (see Figure 1-7).

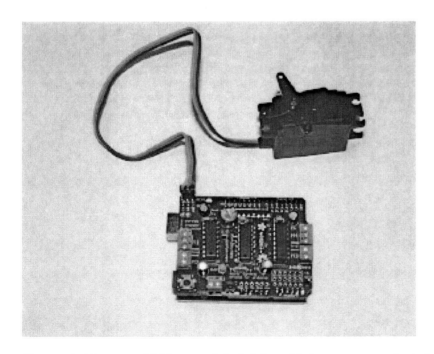

Figure 1-7. *The motor shield on top of the Arduino with the servo motor attached*

In the Blink example, you power the Arduino with the USB cable to the computer. Since this project will eventually be independent of the computer, a battery pack or wall adapter will be required to power the project. If the wall adapter is used, it plugs directly into the Arduino, and the LEGO casing will require a hole the width of one LEGO stud. Some motors will require a second power source due to the power consumption of the motors, but for this project, the single power source will be enough for the Arduino and servo motor.

With the Arduino and motor shield set up, there is one last piece of hardware to connect before programming your project. The Ultimate Machine moves into action when a person flips a switch to turn the machine on. Since the machine needs to be switched on, you need to add a switch. You will take a switch (the one in Figure 1-8 is from Radio Shack), solder wires to it, and plug it into one of the digital ports on top of the motor shield so the machine will know when to activate. Since you are using the shield rather than the Arduino itself, the wires will need to be soldered in place to make a secure connection. One end will be soldered into the numbered pin, the other end will be soldered into one of the ground ports, as shown in Figure 1-9.

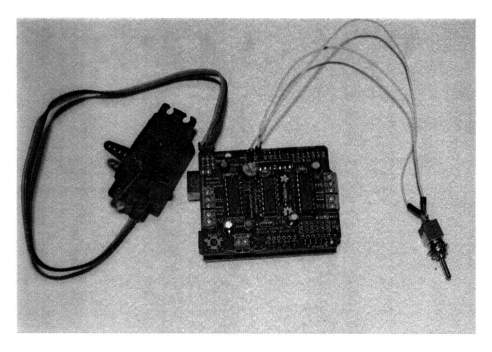

Figure 1-8. *The switch added to the Arduino, motor shield, and motor*

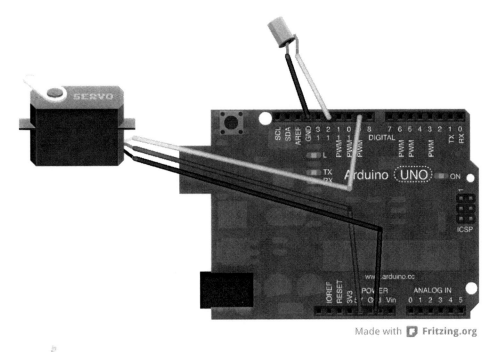

Made with **□ Fritzing.org**

Figure 1-9. *Diagram of the motor and switch connection, as connected without the motor shield*

Programming the Arduino

Once the hardware is completed, it is time to build the software. The program to run the motor is has a similar layout to the program you wrote for the Blink program, but is a little more advanced. The first thing you need to do is include the library for the motor shield. The library includes code that has already been written to drive the motor shield, so you don't have to start from scratch to address the hardware yourself. To install the library, go to www.ladyada.net/make/mshield/use.html and follow the instructions to download and install the motor shield library. Once it is installed and the Arduino software is restarted, copy the code in Listing 1-2.

Listing 1-2. The Ultimate Machine Code

```
#include <Servo.h>

// DC hobby servo
Servo servo1;

// Switch connected to digital pin 2
int SwitchPin = 2;

void setup() {
  // turn on servo
  servo1.attach(9);

  // sets the digital pin 2 as input
  // and enables pullup resistor
  pinMode(SwitchPin, INPUT_PULLUP);
}
```

```
void loop() {
  // read the input pin
  int val = digitalRead(SwitchPin);

  // test if switch has been triggered
  if (val == LOW) {
    servo1.write(115);
    delay(250);
    servo1.write(0);
  }
  delay(100);
}
```

Again, the code is broken into three parts. The first part contains the global variable definitions. Here, you set variables that you want accessible throughout the code. The two include statements at the top of the code include the libraries to interact with the motor. The #include <AFMotor.h> tells the Arduino code that you are going to be using the motor library and the #include <Servo.h> loads the necessary code to use a servo motor. After including them both, you can initialize the servo motor with Servo servo1, which defines the motor and gives it the name servo, which is how you will refer to it as in the rest of the code. Int SwitchPin = 2 sets a number value to SwitchPin, which will be the pin that one end of the switch was soldered into.

In the setup() section, you set up the motor and switch so that you can use them in the loop(). Servo1.attach(9) turns on the servo and tells the code that the servo can be accessed through digital pin 9. pinMode(SwitchPin, INPUT_PULLUP) sets the pin to an input mode to receive digital signals from an external device, in this case a switch. It will be on the port you previously defined in the int statement, so when the switch is active on that port, the code will be able to react.

The third and final part of the code is the loop(). The first thing you need to do is check the status of the switch, so int val = digitalRead(SwitchPin) will put a value in the val variable based on whether the switch is open or closed. The if statement checks the status of the val variable, and if it is LOW, it executes the code within the braces of the if statement. The code will tell the servo motor to move forward 115 degrees with the servo1.write(115) command, then waits 250 milliseconds in the delay(250)command before returning back into the box with servo1.write(0). Once the motor is reset to its initial position, it continues the loop and waits for the switch to be flipped again to turn itself off again.

A typical hobby servo motor can only move 180 degrees, but your motor does not need to move that far to trigger the switch. When building the project, if the motor doesn't move far enough or if it moves too far, adjusting the 115 in the servo1.write() command will adjust how far the motor moves.

Building the Ultimate Machine

Once the Arduino, motor, and switch are set, it's time to build the box to hold it all. The first principle of LEGO building is to build sturdy. Just like in real life, you don't just stack bricks on top of each other, otherwise your buildings would not be sturdy. As seen in Figure 1-10, you stagger your LEGO bricks and cover the seams with bricks, alternating the layout of the bricks in what you are building. This holds the building together and creates a more sturdy framework. It's this sturdiness that allows you to build projects that hold together tightly without needing any glue or extra adhesives for strength.

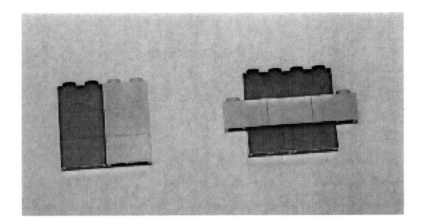

Figure 1-10. *On the left are LEGO bricks stacked one atop the other, while on the right are bricks in a staggered formation. Notice how the bricks cover the seams above and below them, holding the bricks together*

The complete parts list for this project can be found in the appendix.

To give the box a solid foundation, you are going to build the bottom of the box. If you laid out bricks, it wouldn't be very strong and you would need to do a couple layers to give it the tensile strength required to pick up the box and not have the bottom fall out. Instead, you will use plates. When stacking LEGO plates, three plates are the same height as a single LEGO brick, so they can be alternated in your building to cover the seams and still keep the height down by using three plates instead of three bricks. In Figure 1-11, you can see how three plates stack up to be the same height as one brick.

Figure 1-11. *LEGO plates laid out to create the base of your box*

Now that you have decided how you will build the base, you need to figure out the dimensions of the box.

Selecting the Dimensions

The box needs to be at least as wide as the Arduino, and you need to consider how you will fit in the other parts of your build. The Arduino will sit beneath the switch and motor, so you need to figure out the layout of the parts in order to know how big the box needs to be. For the servo to line up to the switch properly the box needs to be approximately 6.5" x 4" or 20 x 12 LEGO studs. In Figures 1-12 to 1-14, you can see how laying out the plates and then crossing over the seams in opposite directions between layers provides a solid foundation that is one brick high.

Figure 1-12. *LEGO plates are laid out to create the base of the box*

Figure 1-13. *The second layer of LEGO plates covers the first layer, but criss-crosses the seams of the first layer to secure them*

Figure 1-14. *The third layer is laid out the same way as the first, locking the plates together*

Building the Brick Walls

Now you can start laying down your bricks. For the first layer, rather than just putting a ring around the edge, you are also bisecting the base to make two rectangles (see Figure 1-15). One rectangle is big enough to hold the Arduino and the motor shield, so that when the box is moved around, the Arduino will not shift. The Arduino should fit in the larger box on the base with only a little bit of extra room. In order to fit a cord to power the Arduino, you should leave a one-brick-width hole in the side of the box. Alternatively, you could attach a 9-volt battery box to the project. If you want to use a battery, you can make a box to hold it as well.

Figure 1-15. *The first layer of the box*

Now you can begin to build up the box over the base you just made. As you lay down the bricks, notice how the second layer covers the seams of the first layer. This will make the box strong enough to support the layers above it and will not break when just picking it up. The next layer, shown in Figure 1-16, will build upon what you have built so far, but cover the seams to strengthen the walls.

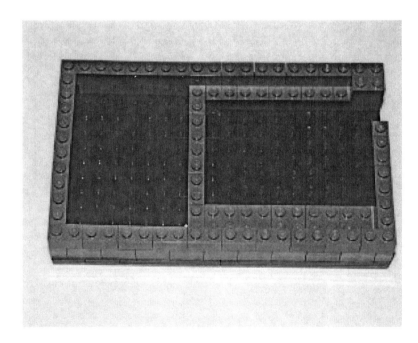

Figure 1-16. *A layer of bricks is added to begin building up the box*

Now add a third layer of bricks to clear the top of the Arduino and motor shield. It's important to make sure that the height of the box's walls clears not only the top of the motor shield, but gives enough room on top for the motor's plug as well to avoid pressure on the shield connection. Again, you should alternate seams to give the box strength to hold the motor and switch (see Figure 1-17).

Figure 1-17. The first three layers of the box, including bricks turned in to create a shelf to hold the motor

Adding The Arduino

With the base of the box completed, it's time to start adding the electronics. The first step is to add in the Arduino in the bottom of the box, as seen in Figure 1-18.

Figure 1-18. *The Arduino is easily seated into the section you made for it*

You can now place a base of plates on top of the box to hold the motor and the switch. You can create a small box to hold it in place. Make sure the small box holds the switch tight, since the motor will be pushing on the switch with a firm amount of force. If the small box breaks or pushes the bricks apart, reinforce the top with plates to give them a firmer grip on the bricks. It is also important to give the wires on the bottom of the switch a way to be fed out of the box; either leave an opening in the first level of the small box or use a LEGO Technic brick and feed the wires out through the hole in the brick, as seen in Figure 1-19.

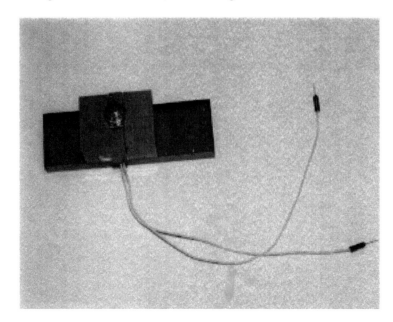

Figure 1-19. *The small LEGO box to hold the toggle switch with the wires fed through a Technic brick*

A platform is then added to hold the toggle switch and servo motor. The switch and motor need to be lined up when the machine is turned on. The motor is lined up with LEGO bricks to keep it in place while you build the rest of the box. It will be made more secure as the walls are built higher, which can be seen in Figure 1-20.

Figure 1-20. The servo motor and toggle switch are laid out on top of stacked LEGO plates and lined up using LEGO bricks

Adding LEGO Arms and a Switch

With the motor and switch in place, the LEGO arms for the motor and switch need to be set up, since that is what will be seen from outside the box. In Figures 1-21 through 1-25, a LEGO Technic beam is secured with a wire to a disc that came with the servo motor, then LEGO Technic beams are added to the top of it, plus a Technic pin with two Technic angle connectors on the ends to give it a wider reach when it comes up to hit the switch. Once that is done, Technic axle joiners are connected by 2M pins to create a pole that the Technic beams can hit with the machine is on, which will just slide over the top of the toggle switch.

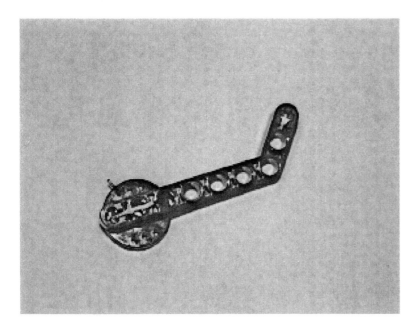

Figure 1-21. *A curved Technic beam is wired to the servo motor's disc*

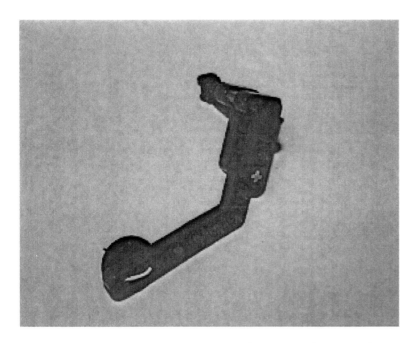

Figure 1-22. *Angled Technic beams are added to the end of the secured Technic beam, and a 5M pin and two angle connectors hold it in place*

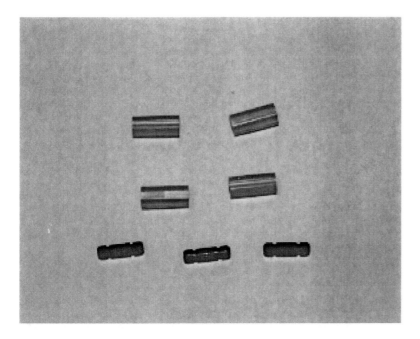

Figure 1-23. *Four axle joiners and three 2M pins extend the switch*

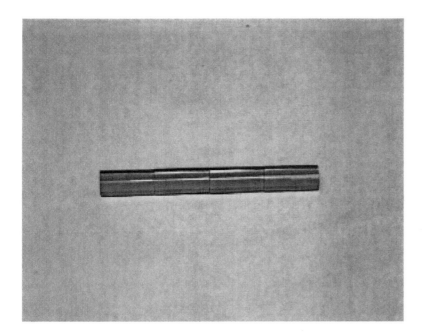

Figure 1-24. *The finished attachment for the switch*

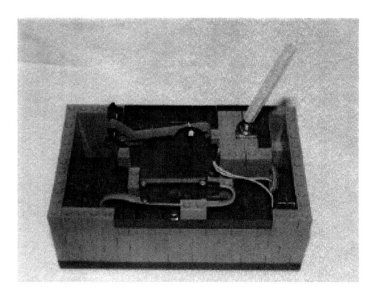

Figure 1-25. *The motor arm and switch extension are added*

Raising the Walls

With the motor arm and switch extension in place, the walls of the box need to be built higher. The walls should be high enough to cover the switch and motor arm. LEGO bricks extend from the walls to cover the bricks holding the motor in place, and another is extended over the motor itself to keep the motor from rising when the arm activates. If there is too much space between the brick above the motor and the servo, fill the space with LEGO plates for a tighter fit. Also note that there are two 2x2 bricks in the top row. These will hold the lid when it is closed to keep it from falling into the box. See Figure 1-26.

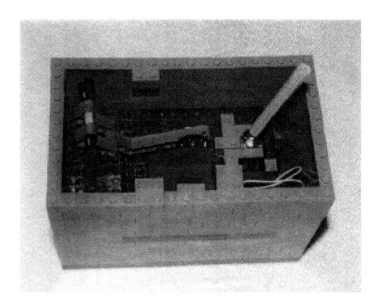

Figure 1-26. *The box extends over the motor and switch*

Building the Lid

Now that the box is prepared, you need to make the lid. Use Technic beams because the rounded ends will make it easier for the box to open and close. Using two pins between each Technic beam will hold them securely and they will not be able to move. Figures 1-27 and 1-28 show the parts and assembly of the lid.

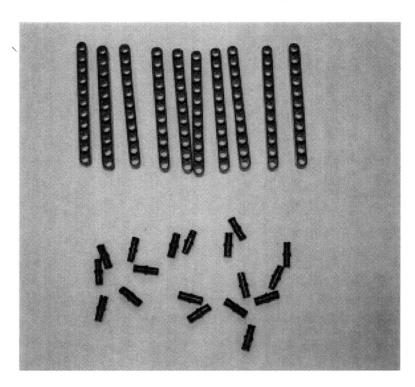

Figure 1-27. *11M Technic beams and black friction Technic beams to hold them together. Two pins should connect between each beam to hold them securely*

Figure 1-28. *The Technic beams connected. There are 2 pins between each beam*

Two Technic bricks with holes in the middle will go on the ends with gray pins to hinge the joint. Use the gray pins there because they are frictionless and allow more movement than the black friction pins. Once the lid is added to the box, a layer of bricks is added around the lid. See Figures 1-29 through 1-32.

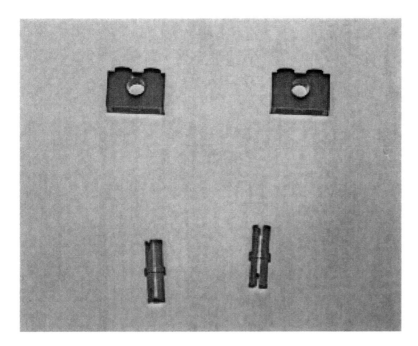

Figure 1-29. *Frictionless pins will go into the 1 x 2 Technic bricks, which will in turn be put into the holes in the end of the beams in the lid*

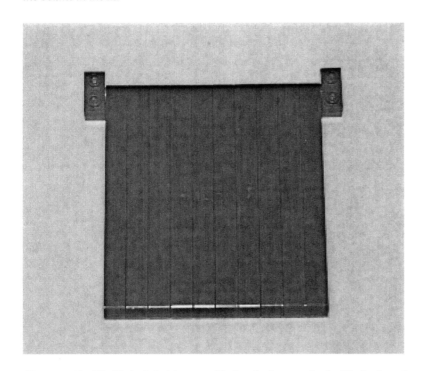

Figure 1-30. *The Technic bricks are added to the beams via the frictionless pins*

Figure 1-31. *The Technic bricks are put on top of the walls of the box*

Figure 1-32. *A layer of bricks is added to border the lid*

With the opening lid completed, all that is left is the cover for the switch. Again, you are going to use stacked plates to cover this part of the box, but you can leave open a slit for the switch. The switch needs to be able to move freely back and forth to turn it off and on. The stick's extension moves easily within a one-stud width and a four-stud length, as seen in Figure 1-33, with the switch shown. It's important to secure the hinge of the box down, as shown in Figure 1-34, so usage of the Ultimate Machine does not lift the lid off the box.

Figure 1-33. *The completed box, ready to turn itself off and on*

Figure 1-34. *The activated Ultimate Machine*

With the switch covered, you have completed your first project. By flipping the switch towards the lid, the machine will be activated and the motor arm will come to life, only to push the switch away from itself and return to its dormant state until it is activated again.

Summary

You just completed an introduction to LEGO building and the Arduino. You learned the basic techniques for using an Arduino, starting from the most basic of programs, making an LED blink, to a more complex one using Arduino shields. You also learned the most basic LEGO building principle of build strong by using a strong base and alternating the bricks to create walls that can support your building. Combining the two gives you the ability to make more interesting projects and give them different levels of activity and interactivity, as you will explore in the following chapters.

CHAPTER 2

▨ ▨ ▨

Using Sensors with the Android

In the last chapter, you made a machine that interacts with itself. A simple response to flipping a switch to turn itself off is a good start, but for more interactive projects, you need to start working with analog sensors that do more than just turn on and off. Sensors allow a machine to monitor the world around it and react accordingly. In this chapter, you will create a project that will be able to react to its surroundings.

When Google introduced their mobile operating system known as Android, they created a mascot to represent it. The little green robot became synonymous with the cell phones and tablets on which the operating system was installed. You are going to create this Android mascot and make him react to his environment. He will be able to "see" what is going on around him and turn to look when things get close within a 180 degree field of view.

A list of the parts in this chapter can be found in the appendix.

The Ultrasound Sensor

There are many different sensors that can be used to send data from the outside world to the Arduino; one such sensor is the ultrasound sensor. An ultrasound sensor sends out a high frequency sound that will bounce off objects and return to the sensor. The time it takes for the sound to go out and bounce back is then calculated to tell the distance of the object. With a simple calculation, it can be converted into a more human relatable value of centimeters or inches. For this Android, you are going to use the PING))) Ultrasonic Distance Sensor by Parallax, Inc., an Arduino-compatible ultrasound sensor.

As seen in Figure 2-1, the PING))) Ultrasonic Distance Sensor has three pins: 5V, GND, and SIG. The 5V and GND pin on the sensor connect to pins on the Arduino, which will allow the circuit to complete and for power to run through the ultrasonic sensor. The SIG or Signal pin can be connected to any of the digital Arduino pins; it's how the data is moved from the sensor to the Arduino itself.

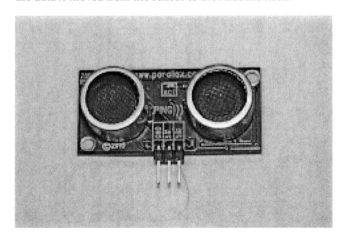

Figure 2-1. *The PING))) Ultrasonic Distance Sensor by Parallax, Inc*

To see how the ultrasonic sensor works with the Arduino, you are going to create a basic program to light an LED light using the ultrasonic sensor. If an object is within a range of 6 inches or less, the LED will light up; otherwise the light will be turned off. First, you need to wire up the sensor, LED, and Arduino, but you will use a breadboard to do your prototyping.

On a breadboard, components that are plugged in on the same horizontal line are connected, so the jumper wires next to the pins are connected to the sensor through the breadboard. On the edge of the breadboard are two lines that run the length of the breadboard and they are connected, but they are meant for power and ground so the different components can share power. A single wire is run from the + and - lines to the 5V and ground pins, which will require less lines run from the parts to the Arduino (see Figure 2-2).

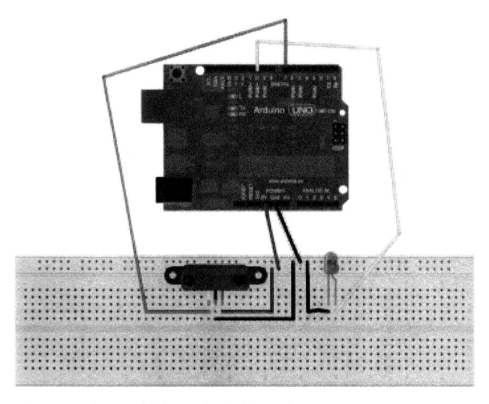

Figure 2-2. *A diagram of the layout of the Arduino and sensor*

As seen in Figure 2-3, the sensor is plugged into the breadboard and three wires are plugged in behind the pins. The wire behind the 5V pin is connected to the column on the edge with the + next to it and the pin for the Ground is connected to the column with the - next to it. The LED is plugged in to breadboard as well, with a wire connected to the negative side (shorter pin) also leading from the LED to the - column, so the LED and sensor can share the ground line.

Figure 2-3. *The Arduino, ultrasonic sensor, and green LED connected to the breadboard*

To connect the breadboard to the Arduino, you need to start by running the power from the Arduino to the breadboard. By running a wire from the + to the 5V pin and another wire from the – to the ground pin, power can be run through the sensor. The signal pin from the sensor is placed in pin 7 and the positive lead from the LED needs to be put in pin 10 on the Arduino. While the placement of the signal and LED pins is arbitrary among the numbered digital pins, these are the pins used in Listing 2-1, which is based on the sample open source code by David A. Mellis and Tom Igoe.

Listing 2-1. PING))) Example Code

```
// sets the constants for the sensor and led signal pins:
const int pingPin = 2;
const int led = 10;

void setup() {
  // initialize serial communication:
  Serial.begin(9600);

  // sets the LED pin to an output mode
  pinMode(led, OUTPUT);
}

void loop() {
  // establish variables for duration of the ping,
  // and the distance result in inches:
  long duration, inches;
```

```
// The PING))) is triggered by a HIGH pulse of 2 or more microseconds.
// Give a short LOW pulse beforehand to ensure a clean HIGH pulse:
pinMode(pingPin, OUTPUT);
digitalWrite(pingPin, LOW);
delayMicroseconds(2);
digitalWrite(pingPin, HIGH);
delayMicroseconds(5);
digitalWrite(pingPin, LOW);

// The same pin is used to read the signal from the PING))): a HIGH
// pulse whose duration is the time (in microseconds) from the sending
// of the ping to the reception of its echo off of an object.
pinMode(pingPin, INPUT);
duration = pulseIn(pingPin, HIGH);

// convert the time into a distance
inches = microsecondsToInches(duration);

// turn on the led if object is within six inches
if (inches < 6) {
    digitalWrite(led, HIGH);
} else {
    digitalWrite(led, LOW);
}

// send the value in inches to the Serial Monitor
Serial.print(inches);
Serial.println(" inches");

// short delay before starting over again
delay(100);
}

long microsecondsToInches(long microseconds) {
    // According to Parallax's datasheet for the PING))), there are
    // 73.746 microseconds per inch (i.e. sound travels at 1130 feet per
    // second). This gives the distance travelled by the ping, outbound
    // and return, so we divide by 2 to get the distance of the obstacle.
    // See: http://www.parallax.com/dl/docs/prod/acc/28015-PING-v1.3.pdf
    return microseconds / 74 / 2;
}
```

In this code, you start by defining the pingPin as the pin the ultrasonic sensor is plugged in to and led as the pin that the LED is plugged in to (7 and 10, respectively). In the setup() function, you open a connection to the computer with the Serial.begin(9600), so that the Arduino can communicate with the computer when it is plugged in via USB cable. The 9600 defines the speed of the communication between the two; you are going to use it to monitor the values passed back from the sensor. You also define the LED pin as output but you don't define the sensor in the setup because the pin connected to the ultrasonic sensor will switch between input and output for sending and receiving the ultrasonic pulses.

In the loop() function, the first thing you want to do is define the variables used for reading data from the sensor. The variable duration will be how many microseconds it takes for the sonar pulse to go out and return, while inches will be for converting those microseconds into distance values. Next, the sensor sends out a brief signal by setting `digitalWrite(pingPin, HIGH);` then stops it with `digitalWrite(pingPin, LOW);`. The sensor is then changed to an input sensor and calculates how long between sending and receiving the signal in the line `duration = pulseIn(pingPin, HIGH)`.

If the Arduino is connected to the computer, then messages are sent to be viewed on the computer from the Arduino. When the program is uploaded and running, click on the Serial Monitor under the Tools menu in the Ardunio software and a white screen will open. The `Serial.print()` and `Serial.println()` functions will allow the code to display information in the Serial Monitor window. In the code, `Serial.print(inches)` prints the value returned from the sensor and `Serial.println(" inches")` prints the word *inches* to the screen and the next text will be on the following line. Putting the word in quotes puts the exact word on screen, while no quotes will put a variable value.

To calculate the duration of time between the time the ultrasonic pulse is sent and when it is received and then turn it into a distance that you can relate to, you need to use a custom function. Just like `loop()` and `setup()` are functions, you are creating a new function `microsecondsToInches()`. The word "long" before the function name in the code allows values to be returned by the functions to where they are called, and in this case they are of the datatype long. A long is a 32-bit number, which also allows decimal places, so a number between –2,147,483,648 and 2,147,483,647 can be returned. The `long microseconds` in the parentheses allows a number to be passed and referred to like a regular variable, but the value of the microseconds variable is passed in the call to the function, in this case duration because it is between the parentheses.

Any processing done within the function is contained within that function. Any change to variables within the function does not impact the rest of the program unless a value is returned. In the function `microsecondsToInches()`, you are doing some fairly simple mathematics, so you are doing the math and returning the value on the same line.

You could do more complex processing and set the value to a variable, then have the code read return variable to export the answer from the variable rather than directly from the line of code. In your function, you are dividing the number of microseconds it takes sound to travel an inch and dividing by two, since the duration takes into account the time it takes the pulse to travel to and from the object the sound waves are bouncing off of and returning that value to the function call.

By testing the code and looking at the Serial Monitor, you can see that it takes about 1000 milliseconds to go approximately 6 inches, which you can use to trigger the LED. You check if the duration is larger than 1000 with an `if` statement, and if it is, you set the LED to turn off; otherwise the `else` statement means the object in front of the ultrasonic sensor is 6 inches or less from the sensor and it will turn on.

Adding Additional Sensors

Now that you have an ultrasonic sensor that will turn on an LED light, you want to be able to add additional sensors, since you want to make the project be able to react to more than just whether or not something is close by. To do this, you need to wire up two additional sensors with LEDs to see how the program will work with three ultrasonic sensors. Figure 2-4 shows how three ultrasonic sensors are wired up on a breadboard to connect to the Arduino, and the finished product is shown in Figure 2-5.

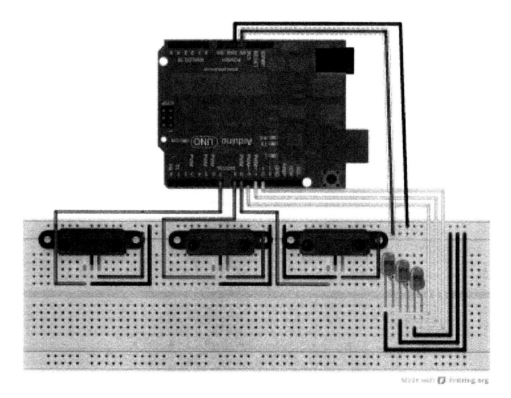

Figure 2-4. *Diagram of the wiring of the Arduino, sensors, and LEDs*

Figure 2-5. *Three ultrasonic sensors connected to an Arduino on a breadboard*

The three ultrasonic sensors connect the same way as the single ultrasonic sensor. The 5V pins each have a jumper wire into the 5V rail and the Ground pins all have jumper wires to the GND rail, as well as the shorter pins on the LEDs. This will let the sensors and LEDs share a single 5V and a single Ground pin among all of them by connecting the 5V and GND with the respective Arduino pins. The sensors plug the signal pins into 7, 8, and 9, while the positive leads on the LEDs plug into pins 10, 11, and 12. Now that you have three sensors and LEDs, you can try altering your code to access them (see Listing 2-2).

Listing 2-2. Running Three Ultrasonic Sensors

```
// sets the constants for each of the sensor and led signal pins:
const int pingPin[] = {2, 3, 4};
const int led[] = {10, 11, 12};

// sets the increment counter for each sensor:
 int counter = 0;

void setup() {
  // initialize serial communication:
  Serial.begin(9600);

  // sets each LED pin to an output mode
  for (int i=0; i<3; i++) pinMode(led[i], OUTPUT);
}

void loop() {
  // establish variables for duration of the ping,
  // and the distance result in inches:
  long duration, inches;

  // resets counter if we run out of sensors
  if (counter == 3) counter = 0;

  // The PING))) is triggered by a HIGH pulse of 2 or more microseconds.
  // Give a short LOW pulse beforehand to ensure a clean HIGH pulse:
  pinMode(pingPin[counter], OUTPUT);
  digitalWrite(pingPin[counter], LOW);
  delayMicroseconds(2);
  digitalWrite(pingPin[counter], HIGH);
  delayMicroseconds(5);
  digitalWrite(pingPin[counter], LOW);

  // The same pin is used to read the signal from the PING))): a HIGH
  // pulse whose duration is the time (in microseconds) from the sending
  // of the ping to the reception of its echo off of an object.
  pinMode(pingPin[counter], INPUT);
  duration = pulseIn(pingPin[counter], HIGH);

  // convert the time into a distance
  inches = microsecondsToInches(duration);
```

```
  // turn on the led if object is within six inches
  if (inches < 6) {
    digitalWrite(led[counter], HIGH);
  } else {
    digitalWrite(led[counter], LOW);
  }

  // send the value in inches to the Serial Monitor for each sensor
  Serial.print("Sensor ");
  Serial.print(counter);
  Serial.print(": ");
  Serial.print(inches);
  Serial.println(" inches");

  // increment counter for the next loop
  counter++;

  // short delay before starting over again
  delay(100);
}

long microsecondsToInches(long microseconds) {
  // According to Parallax's datasheet for the PING))), there are
  // 73.746 microseconds per inch (i.e. sound travels at 1130 feet per
  // second). This gives the distance travelled by the ping, outbound
  // and return, so we divide by 2 to get the distance of the obstacle.
  // See: http://www.parallax.com/dl/docs/prod/acc/28015-PING-v1.3.pdf
  return microseconds / 74 / 2;
}
```

The code to run the three sensors is very similar to the single sensor code; the big difference is using arrays and for loops. An array is a type of variable that can hold a list of values and can be addressed by calling the items in the order they are held. As an example, pingPin is defined as an array in the code because it has the brackets after the name and the values are set in a comma-delineated list between the braces. Since the first address in an array is zero, to retrieve the value 7 from the pingPin array, it would be referred to as pingPin[0]. The zero can also be replaced with a variable, allowing the code to go through the members of the array in order.

By replacing the led and pingPin variables with array variables, you can loop through in setup to define all three LED pins as outputs and in the loop run the sensors in succession to see if there is anything in front of them. You don't want to run them simultaneously to cause interference between the different sensors, but they still run fast enough that it is done in less than a second. Each iteration of the loop() will address a different sensor. By using the counter variable, you can address the sensors in succession, and after the third sensor is checked, it returns to the first one.

You can now use the sensors to light individual LEDs, but that won't make the Android move. Instead, you will add a hobby servo motor and tell it which way to move based on the response from the ultrasound sensors. The Android will turn to look at either side or the front based on stimulus from the sensors. You will use a motor shield again, but this time the sensors signals will be in pins 14, 15, and 16 because the motor shield uses many of the digital pins. While the Arduino itself does not show those pin numbers on it, the pins labeled analog can be defined as digital pins, starting with 14 as analog pin 0. This means that the sensors will be in analog pins 0, 1, and 2. The ends of the 5V and Ground wires can be soldered together and a fourth wire can then be soldered on to have a single wire run from the 5V and Ground pins to the 5V and Ground pins on the motor shield. A diagram of how the sensors connect to the Arduino can be seen in Figure 2-6, and the actual wiring of the sensors can be seen in Figure 2-7.

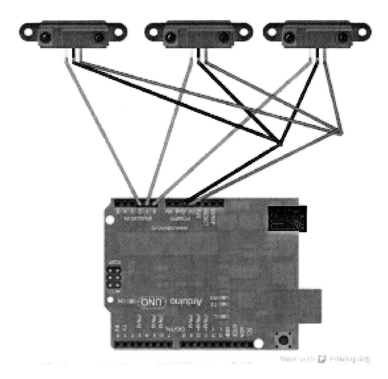

Figure 2-6. *Diagram of the sensors connected to the Arduino*

Figure 2-7. *The ultrasonic sensors soldered to the motor shield on the Arduino*

Once the sensors are connected, the code to utilize them can be seen in Listing 2-3.

Listing 2-3. Running the Servo Motor Based on the Ultrasonic Sensors

```
// include the library for hobby servos
#include <Servo.h>

// DC hobby servo
Servo servo1;

// sets the constants for each of the sensor signal pins:
const int pingPin[] = {2, 3, 4};

// sets the increment counter for each sensor:
int counter = 0;

// sets the speed of the servo movement
int spd = 10;

// sets the left, right, and center positions of the servo
int left = 10;
int right = 170;
int center = (right - left) / 2;

// sets the variable to keep track of the servo angle
int angle = center;

void setup() {
  // initialize serial communication:
  Serial.begin(9600);

  // turn on servo and move to center
  servo1.attach(9);
  servo1.write(center);
}

void loop() {
  // establish variables for duration of the ping,
  // and the distance result in inches:
  long duration, inches;

  // resets counter if we run out of sensors
  if (counter == 3) counter = 0;

  // The PING))) is triggered by a HIGH pulse of 2 or more microseconds.
  // Give a short LOW pulse beforehand to ensure a clean HIGH pulse:
  pinMode(pingPin[counter], OUTPUT);
  digitalWrite(pingPin[counter], LOW);
  delayMicroseconds(2);
  digitalWrite(pingPin[counter], HIGH);
  delayMicroseconds(5);
  digitalWrite(pingPin[counter], LOW);
```

```
// The same pin is used to read the signal from the PING))): a HIGH
// pulse whose duration is the time (in microseconds) from the sending
// of the ping to the reception of its echo off of an object.
pinMode(pingPin[counter], INPUT);
duration = pulseIn(pingPin[counter], HIGH);

// convert the time into a distance
inches = microsecondsToInches(duration);

// moves the servo to the left if left sensor is triggered
if (inches < 6 && counter == 0) {
  if (angle != left) {
    for (int i=angle; i>left; i--) {
      servo1.write(i);
      delay(spd);
    }
    angle = left;
  }

// moves to the center if center sensor is triggered
} else if (inches < 6 && counter == 1) {
  // moves from left to center
  if (angle < center) {
    for (int i=angle; i<center; i++) {
      servo1.write(i);
      delay(spd);
    }
  // or moves from right to center
  } else {
    for (int i=angle; i>center; i--) {
      servo1.write(i);
      delay(spd);
    }
  }
  angle = center;

// moves to the right if right sensor is triggered
} else if (inches < 6 && counter == 2) {
  if (angle != right) {
    for (int i=angle; i<right; i++) {
      servo1.write(i);
      delay(spd);
    }
    angle = right;
  }

// otherwise hold steady at the current position
} else {
  servo1.write(angle);
}
```

```
  // send the value in inches to the Serial Monitor for each sensor
  Serial.print("Sensor ");
  Serial.print(counter);
  Serial.print(": ");
  Serial.print(inches);
  Serial.println(" inches");

  // increment counter for the next loop
  counter++;

  // short delay before starting over again
  delay(100);
}

long microsecondsToInches(long microseconds) {
  // According to Parallax's datasheet for the PING))), there are
  // 73.746 microseconds per inch (i.e. sound travels at 1130 feet per
  // second). This gives the distance travelled by the ping, outbound
  // and return, so we divide by 2 to get the distance of the obstacle.
  // See: http://www.parallax.com/dl/docs/prod/acc/28015-PING-v1.3.pdf
  return microseconds / 74 / 2;
}
```

The code for running the servo motors based on the ultrasonic sensors starts the same way as the code used for the Ultimate Machine. You include the libraries to run the motor and define the servo motor before defining the rest of the variables. Instead of lighting the LEDs when the ultrasonic sensors see an object, you put a value in the array defined as sensor. Arrays are defined by their name followed by square brackets, like variable[ ], and items in it can be addressed with numbers in the brackets. You assign the value zero to all three of the sensor values, so the sensors will start from a state where they have not yet seen anything. In the setup() function, you start the servo and then center the motor so it is looking straight ahead.

For this project, the head will have three positions (left, right, and center). If either of the side sensors is triggered, the motor will turn all the way to that respective side, but if the middle sensor is triggered, it needs to know which side it is facing in order to know which way to turn. Using if else statements, you check the array to see which sensors are triggered and then turn. When a sensor is triggered, it checks whether the last sensor triggered was the same one, and if not, it turns and sets the position variable for the next iteration of the loop. In the code, you have Serial.print statements so you can make sure it all works when connected to the computer before building the Android.

Building the Android

Once you have the code and have tested it, you can start building the Android. The Android's body is made of concentric circles that rest atop each other, with a dome for the head. The arms and legs are made of smaller circular rings that are attached to the main body.

Start with the Foundation

Since the Android is round and LEGO bricks are not, you need to accommodate this by building into as round a shape as you can with the bricks. This is done by having a four stud side and having a two brick spacing to create a step pattern. You also have a brace four bricks wide running through the bottom of the Android to support the legs and the Arduino when you install them (Figure 2-8).

Figure 2-8. *The first layer of the Android's body*

As when building the walls of the Ultimate Machine, you alternate the way the bricks are laid out in the rings for the Android's body. The center row will just have a row of 2 x 4 bricks over the center to lock in the brace. You will add another layer in the step after the one seen in Figure 2-9 underneath the brace to lock it in.

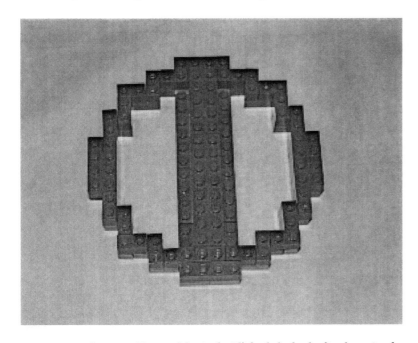

Figure 2-9. *The second layer of the Android's body locks the first layer in place*

When looking at a picture of the Android, the bottom curves inward. You can approximate that look by having a layer beneath the first layer that brings the ring one stud in. The center brace must be reinforced by using an alternate layout that is four studs wide. Figure 2-10 shows what the ring looks like while Figure 2-11 shows what the ring looks like when installed on the bottom of the first ring.

Figure 2-10. *The smaller ring goes beneath the first ring*

Figure 2-11. *The smaller ring placed beneath the two rings that were previously assembled*

The next level of the body will hold the Arduino in place.

Building a Harness for the Arduino

A LEGO harness will be strong enough to hold the Arduino so that nothing else will be needed to hold it. While you already soldered the sensors into the motor shield, they won't be seen in the pictures until the steps in which you begin to place them for clarity when looking at the building process (see Figures 2-12 and 2-13).

Figure 2-12. *The next level of the body creates a harness for the Arduino*

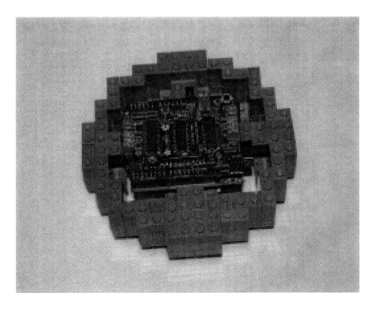

Figure 2-13. *The Arduino is placed into the cradle that was created for it*

Adding a Level for the Power Plug

The next level of the Arduino body will create a space for the power plug connection. The side that has the connection is the back of the Android, so everything else you build for the body will use it as a point of reference. The plug can be seen in Figure 2-14.

Figure 2-14. *The power plug is given a hole in the back of the Android as the fourth layer is added*

Building the Body

In Figures 2-15 to 2-18, the Android's body is built up. The bricks continue to be alternated to build up strength in the walls as the Android grows taller. You lay more concentric rings atop each other, alternating the way they lie on top of each other in order to build a strong body that will be able to support itself.

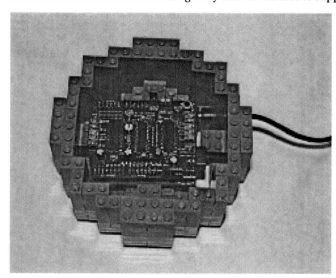

Figure 2-15. *The fifth layer, above the plug, locks it into place*

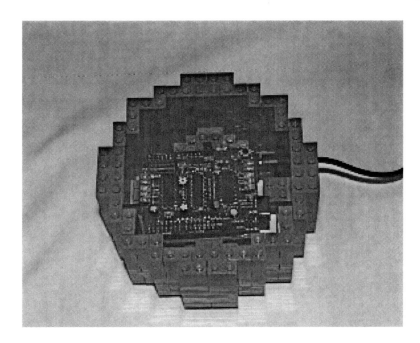

Figure 2-16. *The sixth layer is built on top of the plug*

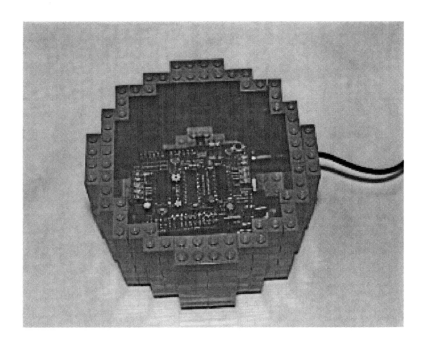

Figure 2-17. *A third layer, the seventh, is built on top of the plug, continuing to alternate the bricks on top of each other*

Figure 2-18. *The eighth layer is built over the plug*

With four layers built over the plug, the fifth layer adds a brick with a hole in the middle in order to add the Android's arms.

Adding Arms and Sensors

The 1 x 2 Technic bricks are placed on the two sides that run perpendicular to the side with the plug sticking out of it, as seen in Figure 2-19.

Figure 2-19. *A layer is added with 1 x 2 Technic bricks to hold the arms*

Once the 1 x 2 Technic bricks are in place, two layers need to be added before you can add the ultrasonic sensors; otherwise, the sensors will continually be triggered by the arms. Figures 2-20 and 2-21 show the two layers building up the walls of the Android's body.

Figure 2-20. *The first layer above the 1 x 2 Technic bricks is added*

Figure 2-21. *The second layer is built above the Technic bricks*

Once the walls of the body are built high enough to clear the arms with the sensors, it is time to add the sensors. In Figure 2-22, the placement of the ultrasonic sensors can be seen. In the picture, the sensor connected to pin 14 is the furthest one seen in the picture, pin 15 is the one across from the plug, and pin 16 is the one closest in the picture. A layer of bricks continues the walls and frames the sensors as well. The PING))) Ultrasonic Distance Sensors are two bricks high, so you need add another layer, as shown in Figure 2-23.

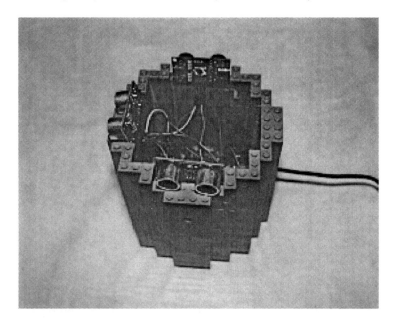

Figure 2-22. The ultrasonic sensors are placed on the body of the Android

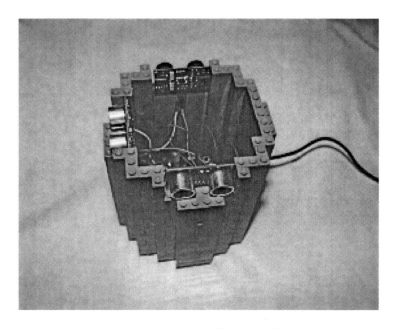

Figure 2-23. A second layer is added to frame the ultrasonic sensors

Once the walls are built up around the sensors, you lock them in using a layer of bricks on top, as seen in Figure 2-24. If there is too much pressure on the sensors when attempting to lock the bricks down on top of the sensors, remove the 1 x 2 brick that is on the inside beneath the sensor to create a groove for the pins to sit in to make space for them. Hanging behind the sensors in the picture is a 1 x 4 brick that helps hold the two 2 x 4 bricks together and keeps the sensors from falling back into the Android. The level covering the sensors is one stud less wide above the sensors, but this is fixed in the level above it, when 1 x 4 bricks are hung down to correct the body shape in this level.

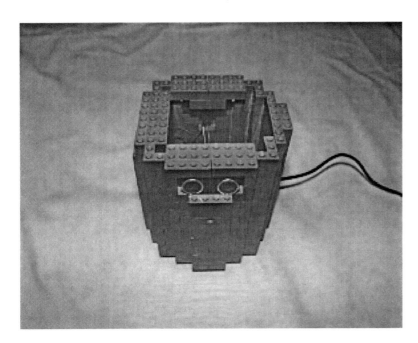

Figure 2-24. *The layer above the ultrasonic sensors covers them*

Separating the Body from the Head

In the Android, a white ring separates the head from the body, so the next level is white. The white level not only rings the body like the previous levels but has bricks turned inwards for two purposes. The bricks turned inwards cover the seams on the covers for the sensors, strengthening them, but they also create a frame to hold the servo motor in place. Figure 2-25 shows the layout of the bricks and the servo motor, but it is not strong enough to hold the motor in place yet.

Figure 2-25. *A layer of white covers the green body to create the Android's neck and holds the servo motor*

When LEGO bricks move on top of other bricks, they will get caught on the studs if not covered. For those situations, there are LEGO tiles that are like LEGO plates—but have no studs on top—in order to create a smooth surface that allows for smooth motion. A ring of tiles covers the white ring of the Android's neck and will lock down the bricks holding the servo motor into place (see Figure 2-26).

Figure 2-26. *A layer of tiles is added to allow smooth movement of the head and to support the servo motor*

Building the Head

With the core body done, the next step is the head. Like the roundness of the body was approximated by stepping the LEGO bricks, the head is a dome that is created using bricks. The first level of the head is similar to the first layer of the Android body; the levels above it recede to give it a roundness. The base of the head does have a thicker ring than the body to allow the narrowing rings to layer on top of it (see Figure 2-27).

Figure 2-27. *The base ring for the Android head*

The second ring of the head shrinks slightly and exposes the corners of the level beneath it. By repeatedly showing the corners on the lower levels beneath them and receding the center of each side, the lower levels begin to get a sense of roundness. Figures 2-28 and 2-29 show how adding two layers starts to give the head a more sphere-like appearance.

Figure 2-28. *The second layer of the head exposes the corners of the first layer*

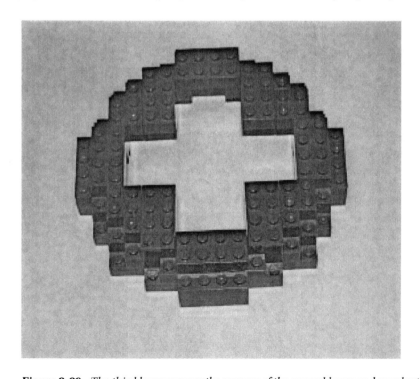

Figure 2-29. *The third layer exposes the corners of the second layer and recedes the edges*

With the fourth layer (Figure 2-30), the edges narrow to studs and expose the corners again. In Figure 2-31, the fifth layer exposes a border of exposed studs and white 1 x 1 bricks to give the Android his eyes, The final level of the head is seen in Figure 2-32 and uses 2 x 4 bricks to cover the hole and 1 x 2 bricks to keep the shape seen in the previous layers.

Figure 2-30. *The edges narrow to two studs as the corners are exposed one more time*

Figure 2-31. *The second-to-last layer leaves a border uncovered from the level beneath it and adds two 1 x 1 white bricks for the eyes*

Figure 2-32. *The final level of the head covers the hole on the top of the head with 2 x 4 bricks and adds four 1 x 2 bricks to keep the shape of the lower levels*

With the head done, you need a way to turn the head. A Technic rod will be used, so a brick needs to be added in order to turn the head.

Turning the Head

To turn the head, use a 2 x 2 round brick with a cross hole in the middle of it that a Technic pin can fit into. To support it, a 2 x 4 plate with holes in it will help lock it into place and allow the pin to fit through. This process can be seen in Figures 2-33 to 2-35.

Figure 2-33. *The bottom of the Android's head*

Figure 2-34. *The round 2 x 2 brick with the Technic hole is placed in the middle. The spaces around it are filled in with 1 x 2 bricks*

Figure 2-35. *A 2 x 4 plate with holes in it is added to support the round 2 x 2 brick*

With the head finished, something needs to be added to hold the head up and make it move.

Supporting the Head

A Technic wheel holding a 5M Technic pin can support the head, but it needs to be attached to the motor. The Technic wheel is wired to an attachment that can connect to the servo motor in order for the motor to be able to turn the wheel.

The Technic pin can then be placed in the wheel construct. Push the attachment, wheel, and pin configuration on the servo, and then turn the servo as far left as it will go to figure out which is the forward face side of the pin. Slide the Technic pin into the hole in the top of the Android's head and the motor will be able to control the head (see Figures 2-36 through 2-39).

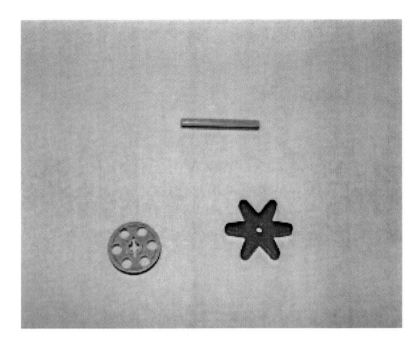

Figure 2-36. *The 5M Technic pin, Technic wheel, and servo motor attachment*

Figure 2-37. *The wheel and the servo motor attachment are wired together and the 5M pin is insterted into the hole*

Figure 2-38. *The attachment is put on the motor. Check which direction the motor is pointing to know which direction the head will face*

Figure 2-39. *The head is placed on top of the Technic pin*

With the head and the body of the Android completed, it needs legs to stand on. The legs will be created like the body was, but on a smaller scale.

Creating the Legs

While the Android will need two legs, Figures 2-40 to 2-46 show how to build a single leg. Repeat the process a second time for the other leg.

Figure 2-40. *The first layer of the Android's leg*

Figure 2-41. *The second layer of the Android's leg*

Figure 2-42. *The third layer of the Android's leg*

Figure 2-43. *The fourth layer of the Android's leg*

Figure 2-44. *To complete the Android's leg, flip it over and place two 2 x 4 green bricks across the middle of the leg to give it a rounded look*

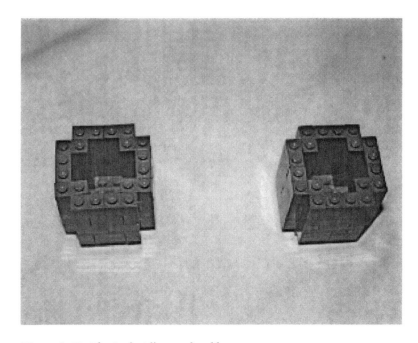

Figure 2-45. *The Android's completed legs*

Figure 2-46. *The Android stands on its new legs. The outer edge of the legs should line up with the outer edge of the lowest level of the Android's body*

With the head, body and legs done, the next step is the arms.

Building the Arms

Building the arms is identical to building the legs, but just taller. While the legs are four bricks high, not counting the 2 x 4 bricks, the arms are eight bricks high. The arms also have 2 x 4 bricks on the top and bottom and a Technic 1 x 2 brick with a hole in it so the arms can connect to the body with a Technic pin. The arms use a black Technic pin because the friction pin will hold the arms in place better than a gray frictionless pin, but the weight of the arms will prohibit them from staying up in certain positions (see Figures 2-47 and 2-48).

Figure 2-47. *The Android's arms, built like the Android's legs, but with a Technic brick and bricks on top*

Figure 2-48. *The Android with the arms attached*

With the arms completed, there is only the Android's antenna left.

Building the Antenna

The Android's antenna is five 1 x 2 bricks high and requires a hinge. You are using green minifigure legs because they give more height and hold their position better than the LEGO hinges, but they can be replaced with a 1 x 2 brick and a 1 x 2 hinge instead of the legs (see Figures 2-49 and 2-50).

Figure 2-49. *The Android's antenna. To the left are the parts required to build the antenna and to the right is the completed antenna*

Figure 2-50. *The completed Android*

Summary

With the Android, you saw how to make the Arduino react to a stimulus more complex than a flipping switch. The three sensors monitor their environment and react accordingly. You also saw how square and rectangular LEGO bricks can be made to emulate a round shape and a dome by their placement near each other.

Now that you have built a reactionary robot, can you improve upon it? You made the Android react to each sensor separately, but what happens if two are triggered at once? Can you make the robot look between the sensors and see things that are not at 90 degree angles?

CHAPTER 3

Twitter Pet

We are entering an era of the "Internet of Things" where everyday objects can connect to the Internet. Is your toast ready? Are your clothes dry? Do your plants need watering? They could each contact you on Twitter or e-mail and send you updates in the near future, if not now.

There are also devices that will monitor the Internet for you, like the Karotz. The Karotz is a rabbit-shaped device that sits on one's desk and moves or flashes lights depending on different online stimulus by connecting to a server or by proximity to a keychain with a radio-frequency identification (RFID) chip, which the Karotz can read and react to. The Arduino can also connect to the Internet and interact, which inspires the next project, a DIY Internet pet inspired by the Karotz.

By using an Arduino, you can allow your LEGO creation to talk to the Internet. Since you will not be setting up a server, you need to make use of an existing server like Twitter. Your LEGO creation could check for searches for hashtags or mentions of a Twitter username, but that requires using a more complex method of connecting to Twitter over a more complex system known as OAuth authorization over the Twitter API. It is simpler to just monitor a Twitter account and check when it tweets, at which point your sculpture will react.

A list of the parts in this chapter can be found in the appendix.

Connecting the Arduino to the Internet

The first thing you need is a way to interact with the Internet from your Arduino. There are two ways to do this: with a shield or with an integrated Ethernet built in to an Arduino. In Figure 3-1, the Ethernet Arduino has an on-board Ethernet port allowing it to talk to the Internet, but no USB on the Arduino, so an external programmer would need to be plugged in to the pins on the top right.

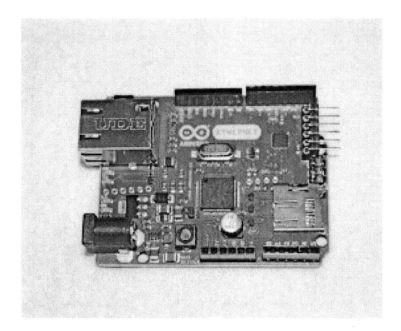

Figure 3-1. *The Ethernet Arduino. The port on the top left is an Ethernet port rather than USB*

Like the motor shield you used previously, the Ethernet shield plugs in directly on top of the Arduino board and can interact and be programmed directly from the Arduino through the pins. The Ethernet shield in Figure 3-2 is the one used in this project and has the same features as the Ethernet Arduino. There are other companies that make similar boards, like Adafruit and Seeed, but they do not have the SD card slot to share and serve files (a feature you will not be using for this project).

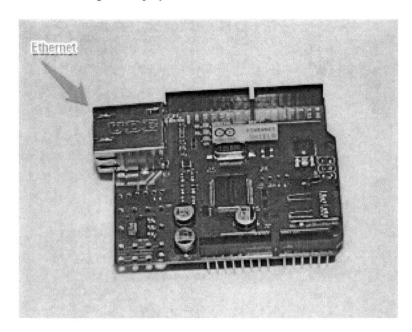

Figure 3-2. *The Arduino Ethernet Shield*

Ethernet makes use of pins 10 to 13 on the Arduino (plus pin 4 if you were to make use of the SD card slot), but you are free to use any of the other pins on the Arduino for your project. Your project will flash LED lights whenever a certain account tweets, so you will put your LEDs on pins 2 and 3 on the Arduino, but you could add more functionality on other pins that are not being used. Listing 3-1 contains the code to access the Internet and communicate with Twitter.

Listing 3-1. Connecting to Twitter and Checking for New Tweets

```
#include <SPI.h>
#include <Ethernet.h>

// Enter a MAC address and IP address for your controller below.
// The IP address will be dependent on your local network:
byte mac[] = { 0x00, 0xAA, 0xBB, 0xCC, 0xDE, 0x01 };
IPAddress ip(192,168,1,20);

// initialize the library instance:
EthernetClient client;

const unsigned long requestInterval = 60000;  // delay between requests

char serverName[] = "api.twitter.com";         // twitter URL

boolean requested;                             // whether you've made a request since connecting
unsigned long lastAttemptTime = 0;             // last time you connected to the server, in
milliseconds

String currentLine = "";                       // string to hold the text from server
String tweet = "";                             // string to hold the tweet
String previousTweet = "";
boolean readingTweet = false;                  // if you're currently reading the tweet

int ledPin = 2;
int ledPin2 = 3;

void setup() {
  pinMode(ledPin, OUTPUT);
  pinMode(ledPin2, OUTPUT);

  // reserve space for the strings:
  currentLine.reserve(256);
  tweet.reserve(150);

 // Open serial communications and wait for port to open:
  Serial.begin(9600);
   while (!Serial) {
    ; // wait for serial port to connect. Needed for Leonardo only
  }
```

```
  // attempt a DHCP connection:
  Serial.println("Attempting to get an IP address using DHCP:");
  if (!Ethernet.begin(mac)) {
    // if DHCP fails, start with a hard-coded address:
    Serial.println("failed to get an IP address using DHCP, trying manually");
    Ethernet.begin(mac, ip);
  }
  Serial.print("My address:");
  Serial.println(Ethernet.localIP());
  // connect to Twitter:
  connectToServer();

}

void loop() {
  if (client.connected()) {
    if (client.available()) {
      // read incoming bytes:
      char inChar = client.read();

      // add incoming byte to end of line:
      currentLine += inChar;

      // if you get a newline, clear the line:
      if (inChar == '\n') {
        currentLine = "";
      }
      // if the current line ends with <text>, it will
      // be followed by the tweet:
      if ( currentLine.endsWith("<text>")) {
        // tweet is beginning. Clear the tweet string:
        readingTweet = true;
        tweet = "";
      }
      // if you're currently reading the bytes of a tweet,
      // add them to the tweet String:
      if (readingTweet) {
        if (inChar != '<') {
          tweet += inChar;
        } else {
          // if you got a "<" character,
          // you've reached the end of the tweet:
          readingTweet = false;
          if (tweet != previousTweet)
          {
            Serial.println(tweet);
            previousTweet = tweet;
        // blink LEDs when there is a new tweet
        for (int i=0; i<50; i++) {
                  digitalWrite(ledPin, HIGH);
              delay(100);
```

```
                digitalWrite(ledPin, LOW);
                delay(100);
                digitalWrite(ledPin2, HIGH);
                delay(100);
                digitalWrite(ledPin2, LOW);
                delay(100);
            }
        }
        // close the connection to the server:
        client.stop();
      }
    }
  }
  } else if (millis() - lastAttemptTime > requestInterval) {
    // if you're not connected, and two minutes have passed since
    // your last connection, then attempt to connect again:
    connectToServer();
  }
}

void connectToServer() {
  // attempt to connect, and wait a millisecond:
  Serial.println("connecting to server...");
  if (client.connect(serverName, 80)) {
    Serial.println("making HTTP request...");
    // make HTTP GET request to twitter:
    client.println("GET /1/statuses/user_timeline.xml?screen_name=justjon&count=1 HTTP/1.1");
    client.println("HOST: api.twitter.com");
    client.println();
    Serial.println("done");
  }
  // note the time of this connect attempt:
  lastAttemptTime = millis();
}
```

The code in Listing 3-1 is based on the sample code for using the Arduino Ethernet by Tom Igoe. Before the setup() function, you include the libraries to be able to control devices and connect to the Ethernet. The MAC address is a unique identifier that defines a machine when it is connected to the Internet and the IP address is an address used by the Internet so that it knows where to find the machine online. An IP address that starts with 198 means it is connected to a local network. The EthernetClient variable is how the code communicates with the Internet to the server defined in the serverName variable, in this case twitter's API server. The rest of the variables are used for holding data and defining the pins that are connected to the LEDs.

In the setup() function, you define the LED pins as output pins and set space for the currentLine and tweet variables. currentLine will hold each line of text as the code reads it in, and tweet will hold the text of the individual tweet from Twitter when it is found in the text received from Twitter. Since they are both strings, they are a series of alphanumeric characters. The line of text you are receiving cannot exceed 256 bytes and a tweet is limited to 140 characters, but you define additional characters to include the XML tag that defines it as a tweet. The Arduino then attempts to get an IP address from the local router or modem that it is connected to, and if it cannot get one, it defaults to using the one defined in the variable definition. Once it has an address, it calls the connectToServer() function to open an initial connection to Twitter's servers.

The connectToServer() function does what the name implies; it attempts to make a connection to the external server defined in the serverName variable, in this case api.twitter.com on port 80. Different services on a computer server have different meanings, and port 80 is means that it is trying to connect to a web server. Client.println is how the code sends commands to the external server, so the HOST is the server it is trying to get data from and the GET is the command that says what information it wants to receive back. The line GET /1/statuses/user_timeline. xml?screen_name=justjon&count=1 HTTP/1.1 tells the Twitter server that it wants to get a status from the defined user's timeline in XML format using the variables screen_name and count, and it wants to receive them back in the Web's 1.1 transfer protocol. The screen_name is defined as justjon, which is my Twitter handle, but it can be changed to any account that you want to monitor. The count variable is set to how many tweets to be returned, but since you want to check for new tweets, you set it to 1 so you are only looking at the most recent tweet. Before ending the function, you track the time of the most recent attempt to connect to the server.

The loop() function first checks to see if it has a current connection to the server with client.connected(), then checks if the data is available with client.available(). If both are found to be true, it begins to read in the response from the Twitter server with the char inChar = client.read(); statement. The code reads in the response from the server one character at a time into the inChar variable. Each of the inChar variables are added to the currentLine variable. If the inChar character is a new line, which is referred to in the code as "\n", then you are done with that line of code and it will reset the currentLine code to be clear for the next line.

The tweet that you are looking for will start with <text> and end with </text>, so a tweet in XML would look like <text>This is a tweet!</text>, and you are checking the line with each new character, so if the currentLine is set to <text>, the code knows that the following characters will be the tweet you are looking for. The readingTweet variable is set to true, so the code knows it is reading the tweet and stores the text in the tweet variable as well as the currentLine. Once it hits the < character, it knows it is hitting the closing </text> tag and that it has grabbed the entire tweet.

Once the entire tweet is read in, the statement if (tweet != previousTweet) compares what is in the tweet variable with the last tweet that was processed, which is blank if it is the first tweet. If the contents of the two variables are not the same, then the previous tweet is set to the current tweet with previousTweet = tweet; and the LED lights are flashed in an alternating pattern 50 times each with the digitalWrite statements before closing the connection to the server to start the process again.

If the server was not connected either due to no previous connection or being closed after reading the tweet previously, then it checks how long it has been since the last connection to the server and subtracts it from the current time, which is also defined in milliseconds. If number of milliseconds between current time and previous connection is greater than the number of milliseconds in the requestInterval, which is defined as 60000 or one minute, then it connects to the server again to read in the latest tweet and repeats the process within the structure of your Twitter animal. Let's build it now.

Building The Twitter Pet

The following sections cover how to build your Twitter Pet.

Building the Base

Your Twitter Pet will not be big enough for the Arduino and Ethernet shield to fit into, so there needs to be a base to hold them in. As with the Ultimate Machine, the base is three layers of overlapping plates forming a solid bottom to hold the Arduino. And like the Android, the body is built from concentric rings of LEGO bricks, but unlike the Android, the rings are of different sizes. Figures 3-3 to 3-5 show the construction of the bottom.

Figure 3-3. *The plates are laid out for the bottom of the box*

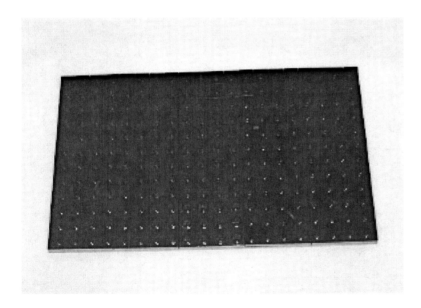

Figure 3-4. *The second layer overlaps the layers of the first, covering the seams*

Figure 3-5. *The third layer lays the same way as the first layer to lock the plates in place*

With the bottom created, the Arduino needs to be placed.

Setting the Arduino in Place

The Arduino and Ethernet shield are held in place by the LEGO, so a partial wall goes through the middle of the box, but the center is left free to allow the wires to pass up through from the box to the sculpture on top. The first level of the walls are shown in Figure 3-6.

Figure 3-6. *The walls of the box are built around the Arduino and hold it in place. Holes are left on the back to allow access to the power and USB plugs*

The box is then built to be high enough to cover the Arduino and the shield. Make the box four bricks high, and alternate the bricks to lock them in and build a solid base. The exception is between the USB and power plugs, where 1 × 2 bricks are stacked atop each other but are locked into place when the bricks are placed on top of it. Figures 3-7 through 3-9 show the construction of the box around the Arduino and the shield.

Figure 3-7. *The second layer covers the first, shifting the bricks to cover the seams*

Figure 3-8. *In the third layer, there is a 1 × 4 brick connecting the 1 × 2 bricks between the plugs to the wall to the left. While the rest of the walls are 2 studs thick, the shield blocks the second row of studs and will be covered in the next step*

Figure 3-9. *The box is built up to solidly hold the Arduino and shield in place. The hole for the Ethernet port will be covered by the lid*

Covering the Arduino

With the box built, it needs to be covered to support the creation on top. The lid of the box is built similarly to the bottom, but has a hole in the middle to run wires through to make the pet interactive. The hole starts wide in Figure 3-10 and is closed tighter in Figure 3-11 before being secured in Figures 3-12 and 3-13. Note that while the wires are not shown in the figures for the lid or during much of the building of the sculpture to make it easier to see the construction, it is much easier to plug the LEDs in now and build around them rather than later once all the LEGO bricks are in place.

Figure 3-10. *LEGO plates are laid out over the top of the box. While they do not cover the enitre top yet, they cover enough to support the next layer*

Figure 3-11. *The second layer of plates covers the first layer and tightens the hole to the size of a 4 × 4 plate. The sculpture on top of it will cover the hole when you begin building*

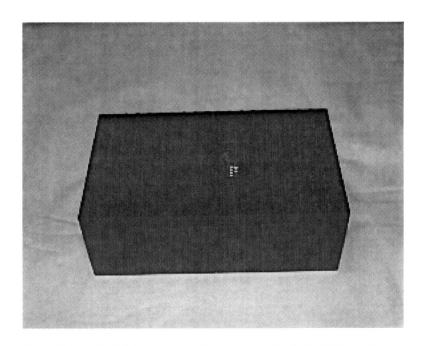

Figure 3-12. *The third layer covers the second and locks the lid into place*

Figure 3-13. *The back of the box shows how the Ethernet, USB, and power ports are easily accessible*

Adding Rings

The Twitter Pet is made of concentric rings that rest on top of the box. There are five sets of rings that stack atop each other to build the Twitter Pet's body. There is a single ring with a larger ring that is two bricks high atop it, followed by the widest ring that is four bricks high before bringing it back in to a smaller ring that is three bricks high, then finally the head, which is four bricks high.

The First Ring

The first ring is the smallest one, covering the hole and simulating roundness with a diamond pattern that will be built upon with the rings that stack on top of it. The first ring can be seen in Figure 3-14.

Figure 3-14. *The smallest, diamond-shaped ring*

The Second Ring—Two Bricks High

The second ring expands on the first, creating two layers that form the next level of the sculpture. The expanding layers give it a slightly rounded look as it grows upwards. The two studs at the edges go out two studs and there is a border that goes around the diamond, as shown in Figure 3-15.

Figure 3-15. *The second level expands out from the first*

The Third Ring—Four Bricks High

Figure 3-16 shows the second level of the same width that gives it height and secures it in place.

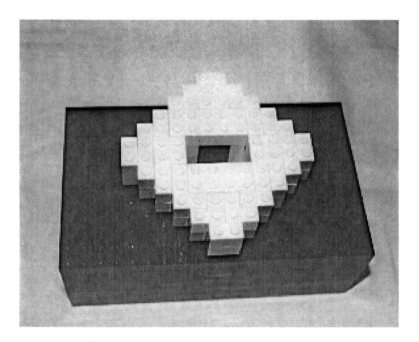

Figure 3-16. *The third level alternates from the second to lock it into place*

With the completion of the third level, you now build the widest part of your creation, the fourth ring.

The Fourth Ring—Four Bricks High

The fourth ring expands the edges out one stud and creates a border around the previous ring, except where the edges push out. In Figure 3-17, there are bricks from the following level in place. These hold up the pieces that have no support underneath them. They are locked in as the levels above it are built. Figures 3-18 through 3-20 show the stacking of the widest part of the sculpture. Notice how 1 × 2 bricks from the level above the current one being built hold the pieces in place. Since LEGO bricks cannot float in space, they are put there to hold the bricks in place during the building of that level and are secured when the level above it is added.

Figure 3-17. *The fourth layer starts the widest part of the pet*

Figure 3-18. *The fifth layer is filled in to support the layer beneath it*

Figure 3-19. *A third layer of the widest ring is laid down*

Figure 3-20. *Fourth and final of the widest rings*

The Fifth Ring—Three Bricks High

With four levels done, you start to bring in the rings inwards to give it a somewhat egg shape. The next set of rings matches the two rows of rings below the widest set of rings, but are stacked three high instead of two to make the top of your creation taller than the bottom. As in Figure 3-17, Figure 3-21 shows the level above it being used to hold the bricks in place until they are secured by the level above them. Figures 3-22 and 3-23 show the building of the set of rings on top of the widest set of rings.

Figure 3-21. *A smaller ring is brought in to make the body less wide at this point. 1 × 2 bricks are used to hold the bricks in place until they are secured in the next step*

Figure 3-22. *The second level of this width is filled in*

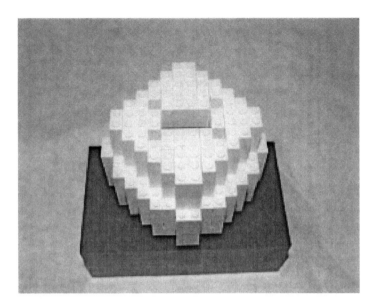

Figure 3-23. *The third and final layer is locked in on top of the previous two layers of this width*

Adding the Eyes and Nose

The next level of the Twitter Pet is the same width as the original diamond shape on the lowest ring above the box, but on top it will be four levels high and will give your pet some personality. In Figure 3-24, you prepare the eyes and nose. Using 1 × 2 Technic bricks with a single hole in the middle, you can push LEDs through two of them and a 1 × 1 round into the third as a nose. Although a standard LED should fit into the hole, if it does not, the wires can be run through the hole and the LED can stick out on one side.

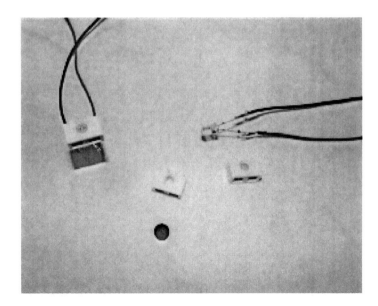

Figure 3-24. *Three 1 × 2 Technic bricks with LEDs for the eyes and a 1 × 1 round for the nose*

With the eyes and nose prepared, you can start building the head.

Adding the Head

Although the head will be four rows high, you can adjust it for the eyes, nose, and ears. The first two levels are done like the previous rings, although, smaller; the two that follow are modified to give your pet some personality, as shown in Figures 3-25 and 3-26.

Figure 3-25. *This ring is identical to the one at the bottom of the pet*

Figure 3-26. *This ring overlaps the one in front of it, but the front edge has the 1 × 2 Technic brick with the 1 × 1 round in it*

In the next level, you make space for the ears and put in the eyes. The two studs that are the sides are left open to put the ears in. Additionally, the front two studs that fill out the diamond are left out to show the four stud width of the two Technic bricks that have the eyes. This can be seen in Figure 3-27.

Figure 3-27. *The next level puts the eyes in place and leaves open holes for the ears*

Your pet's ears are made from Technic beams. Two 7M beams make up the ears and they're held together with a 3M beam and two black Technic pins. Using black Technic pins allow the ears to be posed once they are in your pet's head and they hold their place. Figure 3-28 shows the pieces for the ears and Figure 3-29 shows how it is assembled.

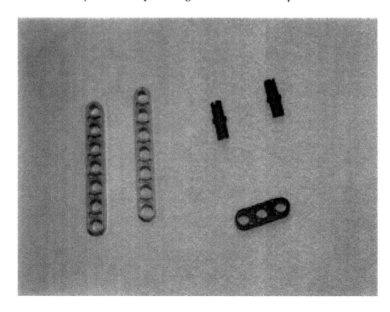

Figure 3-28. *Two 7M beams, a 3M beam, and two black friction pins make up the ears*

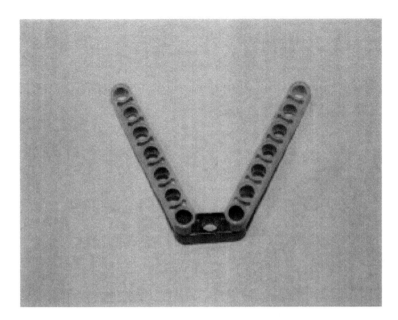

Figure 3-29. The assembled ears

The next level of the pet's head have the corners placed, but leave a two-stud opening coming in from all sides so that the ears can extend from the head and can be locked in with 2 × 4 bricks (see Figures 3-30 and 3-31). The ears slide down into the hollow head, but if the wires impede the ability to slide it in, push the wires down out of the way—but make sure that none of the exposed parts of the wires come in contact with each other or the electricity will seek out the path of least resistance and the LEDs will not light up.

Figure 3-30. The corners are built up one level and the ears are lowered into the open head

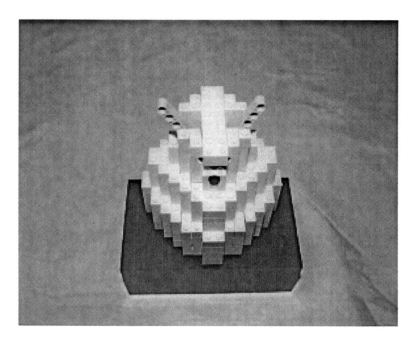

Figure 3-31. *Two 2 × 4 bricks are placed on top to lock the ears into place*

The final step is to place two 2 × 4 bricks side by side on top. This locks the bricks in place and gives a rounded look to the top of your pet's head. The final step can be seen in Figure 3-32.

Figure 3-32. *Two 2 × 4 bricks are placed on top of your pet, completing it*

Summary

The Internet is a fount of information, and with an Arduino and an Ethernet shield or on-board Ethernet, your pet can interact with the world around it, from Twitter to e-mail to anything else with any API or RSS feed. Your basic robot is able to tell when a person tweets and responds by flashing its LED eyes.

What else can you make the Twitter Pet do? Can you make it respond to certain hashtags or mentions of a Twitter account? Can you have it alert you when you have new e-mail? Can you have it let you know when your favorite web site is updated? Can you make it do additional things? The possibilities are as limitless as the amount of information on the Internet.

CHAPTER 4

■ ■ ■

RFID and the Crystal Ball

Many objects these days are tagged electronically. When leaving a store, it's possible that an alarm will go off if you leave with an item that still has a tag on it. A purchase can be made by waving a tag over a credit card machine. These technologies use radio-frequency identification (RFID) to tag and track items based on a chip placed on an item and a device that can read it. You can use this technology to trigger reactions in your LEGO creations, like the crystal ball you are going to build in this chapter.

The RFID chip contains a radio-frequency electromagnetic field coil that modulates a magnetic field that can transfer a unique identification code to a reading device. The RFID chip itself does not require any power and can be embedded into a box, a piece of plastic, or even a person. When the RFID tag is placed in proximity to the RFID reader, the tag powers up and sends its unique identification number back to the reader, which in this case will be processed by the Arduino. You will use RFID to trigger the crystal ball and you will even make sure that only your wand will trigger it—and not those of evil wizards.

Arduino and RFID

Figure 4-1 shows two RFID chips; they can be purchased from SparkFun and used by an RFID receiver. The 125khz tags are two different sizes and shapes and can be used for different projects. The one on the right is about the size of a grain of rice and is the one used in this project. The advantage of the button RFID tag on the left is that it is able to be read from a larger distance of 32mm, compared to 10mm, due to its larger size and the size of the antenna within it.

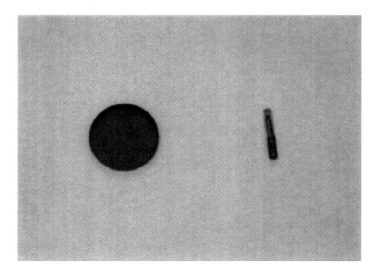

Figure 4-1. *SparkFun button and glass capsule RFID tags*

The RFID reader you will be using is the ID Innovations RFID Reader ID-12, which is available from SparkFun. It is compatible with the Arduino and can read RFID tags up to 100mm away from the reader. The ID-12 has a unique pin spacing of 2mm between pins, which is narrower than the 0.1" used by breadboards, and has thinner pins. Because of this, it is best to solder the ID-12 to a breakout board that will adjust the spacing and make it easier to work with the RFID reader. Figure 4-2 shows the ID-12 and its breakout board.

Figure 4-2. *On the right is the Sparkfun ID-12 RFID reader and on the left is the breakout board that will make it easier to work with the Arduino and a breadboard*

Figure 4-3 is a diagram of how the RFID reader is connected to the Arduino, and Figure 4-4 shows the ID-12 RFID reader connected to an Arduino via a breadboard. Five pins are used by the Arduino on the RFID reader. Pins 1 and 7 connect to the Ground connection on the Arduino, pin 11 connects to the 5V pin, pin 2 on the RFID reader connects to pin 13 on the Arduino, and pin 9 on the RFID reader connects to pin 0. There is also an LED connected to pin 3 for testing purposes.

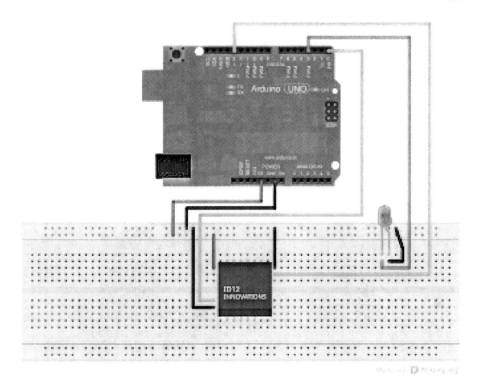

Figure 4-3. *A diagram of how the RFID reader connects to the Arduino*

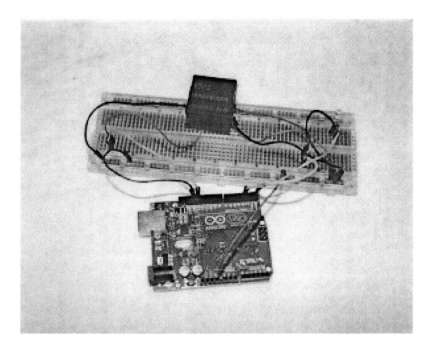

Figure 4-4. *The RFID reader is connected to the Arduino via a breadboard*

While the RFID reader communicates with the Arduino using pin 0, so does the computer when uploading a program. Since they both utilize the same pin, when uploading the sketch to the Arduino, the wire must be removed or the computer will give an error.

The RFID reader and the Arduino are connected on a breadboard in Figure 4-3 in order to test out the wiring and the program in Listing 4-1. When you actually install the hardware into the LEGO, you will be doing it without the breadboard.

Now that the basic wiring has been laid out, you need to program your Arduino. Since every RFID tag has a unique identifier, I cannot program for particular RFID tags, but the code supplied here does print the tag's unique identifier to the serial monitor when connected to the computer. Adjusting the code to accept only particular RFID tags or to react differently to different RFID tags just requires some if statements.

▒ **Note**   I won't delve into the process of getting the codes off the RFID; the seeds are planted in the code and you can extrapolate it out.

Generating Magic with Code

Once the Arduino and the RFID are wired together, it will require code to drive the crystal ball and have it interact with the magic wand. Listing 4-1 shows how to program the Arduino to allow them to interact. Special thanks to Brian Evans for assistance with this code.

Listing 4-1.   Crystal Ball

```
#include <SoftwareSerial.h>

SoftwareSerial rfid(2,3);

int ledpin[] = {3, 5, 6, 9, 10, 11};
int ledcount = 6;

char tag01[] = "4500B8F08489";
char tag02[] = "4500B8D36947";

char tagString[13];

void setup() {
  Serial.begin(9600);
  rfid.begin(9600);
}

void loop() {
  if (rfid.available()) {
    if (getTag()) {
        printTag();
        for (int numval=0; numval < 4; numval++) {
            for(int value = 255; value >=100; value=value-5) {    // fade out (from max to min)
                for (int i=0; i<ledcount; i++) {
                  analogWrite(ledpin[i], value);                  // sets the value (range from 0 to 255)
                }
```

```
                    delay(30);
                }
            delay(500);
            for(int value = 100 ; value <= 255; value=value+5) { // fade in (from min to max)
                for (int i=0; i<ledcount; i++) {
                    analogWrite(ledpin[i], value);            // sets the value (range from 0 to 255)
                }
                delay(30);              // waits for 30 milli seconds to see the dimming effect
            }
            delay(500);
        }

        for(int value = 255; value >=0; value=value-3) {  // fade out (from max to min)
            for (int i=0; i<ledcount; i++) {
                analogWrite(ledpin[i], value);               // sets the value (range from 0 to 255)
            }
            delay(30);
        }

        for (int i=0; i<ledcount; i++) {
            analogWrite(ledpin[i], 0);          // sets the value (range from 0 to 255)
        }

    }
  }
}

boolean getTag() {
  char startByte = rfid.read();
  delay(20);

  if (startByte == 2) {
    int index = 0;
    while (index < 12) {
      char incomingByte = rfid.read();

      tagString[index] = incomingByte;
      index++;
    }
  }
  rfid.flush();
  return true;
}

void printTag() {
  for (int i=0; i<12; i++) Serial.print(tagString[i]);
  Serial.println(compareTags());
}
```

```
const char* compareTags() {
  if (strncmp(tag01, tagString, 12) == 0) return " Tag 1";
  else if (strncmp(tag02, tagString, 12) == 0) return " Tag 2";
  else return " Not recognized.";
}
```

Before you create the setup() function, you set up some variables, most notably the LED array. Pins 3, 5, 6, 9, 10, and 11 are marked on the Arduino Uno as PWM and have a ~ next to their numbers. This denotes them as the analog out pins. Unlike the other pins, which are either high or low, the PWM pins can have a value between 0 and 255. This gives them a lot more flexibility in what they can do and how they can be used. In this program, you will use them to dim LEDs in response to the RFID tags.

There isn't much that needs to be prepared in the setup() function for this program. You are opening a serial connection to the computer so that you can monitor the code on the Arduino compiler's serial monitor and you are opening a connection from the Arduino to the RFID reader, but otherwise there is nothing to execute prior to the loop() function.

The loop() function starts by checking for incoming data with the rfid.available() function call. If there is data, it calls the getTag() function, which reads in the data byte by byte and stores each character in a string. If it is not empty, then it calls the printTag() function, which reads in the tag in front of the RF-ID reader then calls compareTags() to see if it is one of our predefined tags then returns to the calling function and printing to the serial monitor the results.

Once the data is shared on the screen, the LEDs for the crystal ball are lit up. Since it's using the analog out pins, the lights will gradually light up and fade four times before completely fading out again and resetting the number of bytes read from the tag to restart the process. The loop is then restarted to read the next RFID tag.

Since you display the tag value to the serial monitor, it is easy to adjust the code to other tag values than the ones defined in Listing 4-1. After testing the code, change the values in tag01[] and tag02[] to the values from other tags to make it interact with those tags. Any tags that are not defined in the code will not trigger the crystal ball, which mean that other wizards will not be able to use their wands on it.

Building the Crystal Ball

With the code done, it is time to build the crystal ball. The sphere you are going to build to be your crystal ball will be slightly bigger than a softball, but it will require a base to hold the Arduino and the RFID reader so it is more secure and doesn't roll around.

■ **Note** For a complete list of required parts, refer to Appendix A.

Building the Base

The base you will be creating is similar to the one you built for the Twitter Pet, but with some variations. In Figure 4-5, three layers of plates create the bottom of the base and a layer of bricks holds the Arduino in place. The 2 x 2 brick behind the RFID reader has two studs open for the reader to sit in but is loose so there is no pressure on the reader's pins. There are also red bricks in front of the reader to mark the location of the reader, and while it will be a simple red cross, it can be done more ornately.

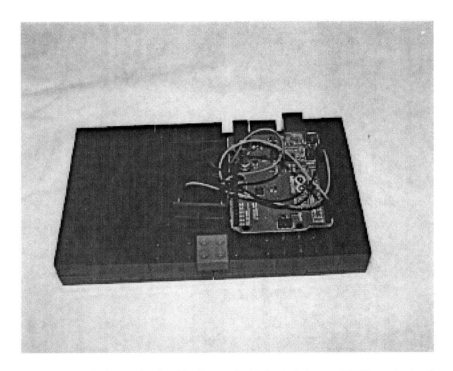

Figure 4-5. *The lowest levels of the base to hold the Arduino and RFID reader in place*

The second layer of the box builds up the first layer and locks it in while securing the first layer by covering the seams, as shown in Figure 4-6. The second layer of the 2 x 2 brick behind the RFID reader is covered with a 2 x 3 brick to lock it into place without putting any pressure on the pins, since the two studs will fit neatly between the pins on the sides going to the Arduino and the pins on the top and bottom that are soldered from the RFID reader into the breakout board.

Figure 4-6. *The second layer of the base secures the first layer and locks the RFID reader into place*

A third layer is needed, since the second layer is not tall enough to cover the RFID reader. The column behind the RFID reader is covered by a 2 x 2 brick so it does not put any pressure on the top pins. This column is secured in place when the lid is built on top of the base. Figure 4-7 shows the third layer.

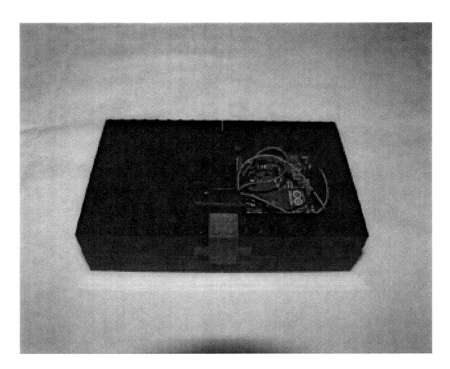

Figure 4-7. *The third and final layer of the base*

Building the Lid

Also like the Twitter Pet, the lid has a hole in the top to allow the LEDs to run from the Arduino in to the cube. The LEDs aren't shown in Figures 4-8 through 4-10 for clarity in seeing how the plates are laid out to leave the middle open. In the first layer, in Figure 4-8, the plates do not cover the column holding the RFID reader in place. This is fixed in the second layer. A 2 x 2 plate is placed on top of the 2 x 2 brick so that it will be even with the first layer and will be secured as the layers are built up.

Figure 4-8. *The first layer of the lid leaves a wide hole that does not secure the column behind the RFID reader*

Figure 4-9. *The second layer is able to lock in the first layer and the column with a plate on top of the 2 × 2 brick*

Figure 4-10. *The third layer of the lid secures it in place while leaving a hole in the middle for wires*

With the base finished and stable enough to support the crystal ball on top of it, you're going to put the lowest level on the base.

Normally the base of a sphere of this size would have a surface of 4 x 4 brick, most commonly done with two 2 x 4 bricks, but since you want to be able to run wires into the sphere, you will create a border of bricks that is four studs on each side and run the wires through it, as shown in Figure 4-11.

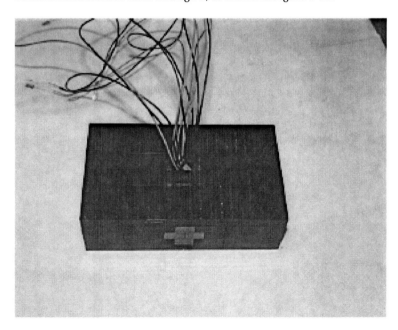

Figure 4-11. *The base of the sphere is a ring that encircles the opening of the base; the LED wires are run through it*

▪ **Note** It's important that the bricks of the sphere are all translucent. In the figures, the sphere is made of translucent blue bricks and the LEDs are ultrabright red LEDs, which can be found at SparkFun. If the bricks are not translucent, no light will be able to escape from within the sphere. It's also recommended to use ultrabright LEDs because the light will be diffused by the bricks and you want as much light as possible to be seen when the crystal ball is activated.

Building the Sphere

Now you need to build the sphere. It is easier to build a sphere starting with the middle and working the way down to create the lower half of the sphere, rather than building upwards from the base. So start with the bottom half of the sphere and then complete the top half.

Assembling the Bottom Half of the Sphere

In Figure 4-12, the center of the sphere is laid out in a ring of 2 x 2 translucent blue bricks. The bricks are stud side down since the studs will point to the top of the sphere.

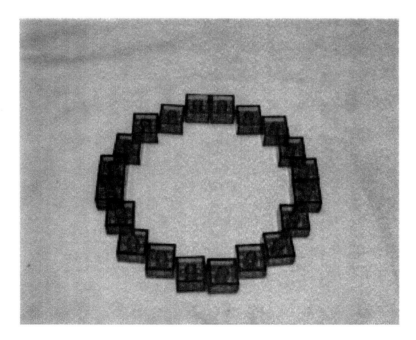

Figure 4-12. *The center ring of the sphere with bricks studs down*

The next ring is the same diameter as the center ring but pulls in the corners. There are three exposed stud holes on each edge where the corners of the 2 x 2 bricks stick out from the ring you are currently building. The four stud sides stay in the same place but are alternated to cover the seams and make the layers stronger, as shown in Figure 4-13.

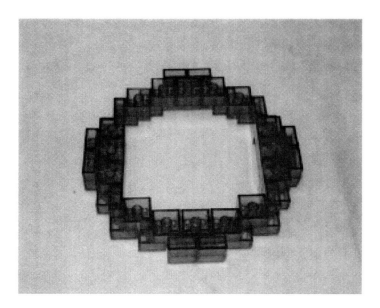

Figure 4-13. *The second ring for the bottom half of the sphere*

The third ring pulls the four stud edges in by one stud to shrink the diameter of that layer. The four corners on each of the sides expose a stud hole from the layer above it. Figure 4-14 shows how the layer should look on top of the second layer.

Figure 4-14. *The third layer pulls the diameter in one stud and exposes the four corner studs on each edge*

In Figure 4-15, the fourth layer keeps the diameter of the third layer but reduces the width of the side edges from four studs to two. There are now five exposed stud holes on the corners of the bricks, including the ones next to the two stud edges.

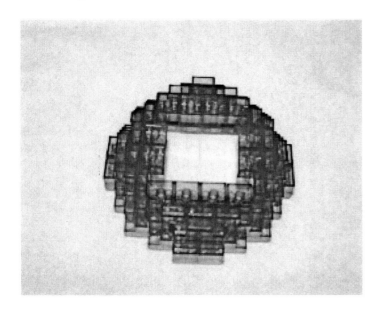

Figure 4-15. *The fourth ring of the sphere*

The fifth ring of the bottom half of the sphere brings the diameter of the ring in one more stud and creates a diamond pattern that overlays the fourth ring. A zigzag pattern is visible in the fourth ring around the diamond pattern. The fifth ring can be seen in Figure 4-16.

Figure 4-16. *The fifth layer of the sphere begins to give it a rounder shape*

The sixth layer is a smaller diamond than the one above it, and the last layer for the bottom of the sphere. The outer edges come in two studs and the second row is four studs wide. Two parallel sides have a width of one stud and the two sides that are perpendicular to those sides are a width of two studs. This can be seen in Figure 4-17.

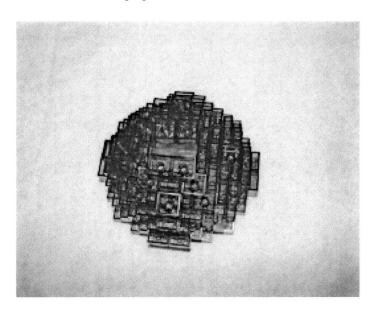

Figure 4-17. *The last ring of the bottom of the sphere*

When you flip over what you have built so far, you have what looks like a translucent LEGO bowl with a hole in the bottom. Insert 1 x 2 bricks to fill to cover the seams and strengthen the integrity of your bowl. The flipped-over half sphere can be seen in Figure 4-18.

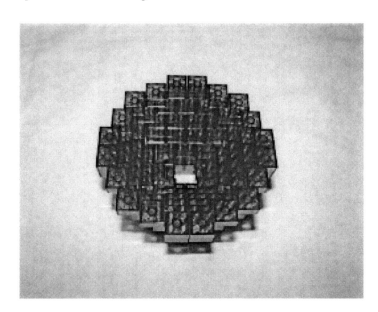

Figure 4-18. *The flipped-over half sphere*

Adding the Bottom of the Sphere to the Base

With the bottom half of the sphere done, it's time to put it on the base. The wires and LEDs should be pulled through the hole and the seams should be lined up over the ring of bricks that were placed on top of the base so that the seams do not line up, in order to strengthen the sphere. Figure 4-19 shows the bottom half of the sphere on top of the base with the LEDs in place. Notice that the wires are of different lengths to shine the lights on different areas of the spheres, and the 22 gauge wires are thick enough to both plug directly into the Arduino and hold the LEDs in place.

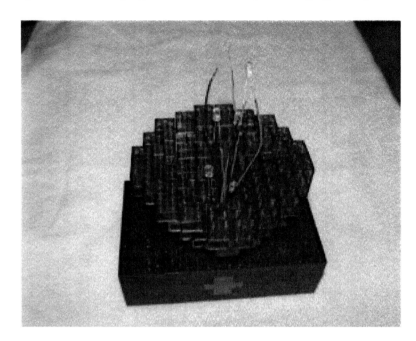

Figure 4-19. *The bottom half of the sphere is secured to the base and the LEDs are arranged*

Completing the Top Half of the Sphere

Now that the bottom half of the sphere is secured to the base, it's time to copy everything you did on the bottom half to the top. Just like the ring below the center ring, the ring above the second ring will have the same diameter as the ring below it and keep the four stud edge, but will expose the corner studs on each diagonal between the outer edges, as shown in Figure 4-20.

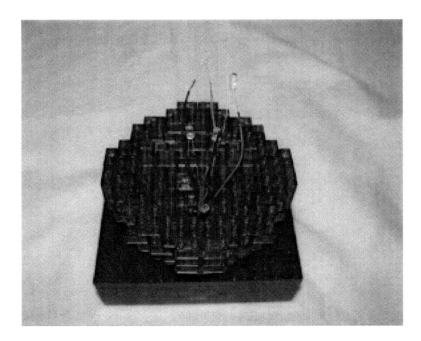

Figure 4-20. *A ring is added above the center ring*

The next ring brings the diameter of the ring in one stud while keeping a four stud width on the edges. Four corner studs will be showing on each edge from the ring below it, as shown in Figure 4-21.

Figure 4-21. *The second layer above the center ring*

Keeping the same diameter as the ring below it, the edge shrinks from four studs to two. Below this ring, five studs are now exposed by the shrinking ring. Figure 4-22 shows the sphere slowly closing up and the LEDs shifted into place to glow when the sphere is done.

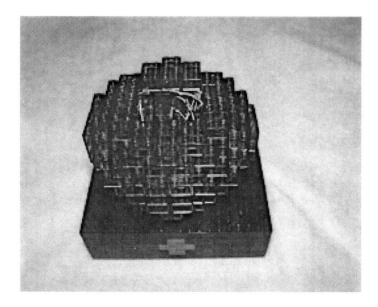

Figure 4-22. *The third layer above the center ring*

The fourth layer above the center ring brings the diameter in another stud and begins to create the round shape on top. Figure 4-23 shows a zigzag pattern that is left visible from the layer beneath it. The center hole is also brought in tighter to support the level above it.

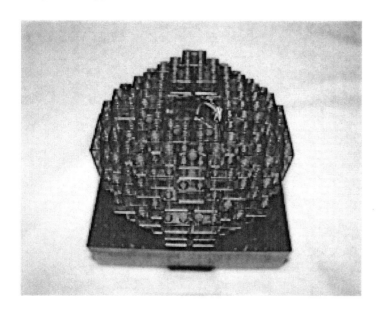

Figure 4-23. *The fourth layer above the center ring, and the first diamond*

The second-to-last layer is a smaller diamond that has a diameter two studs shorter than the diamond beneath it. A full ring of studs ring the diamond pattern and the hole in the middle is tightened up to be able to be covered in the final layer, which is 4 x 4 studs, similar to the bottom of the sphere, but without the hole to run the wires through. The final two layers of the sphere are shown in Figures 4-24 and 4-25, and the completed crystal ball is shown in Figure 4-26.

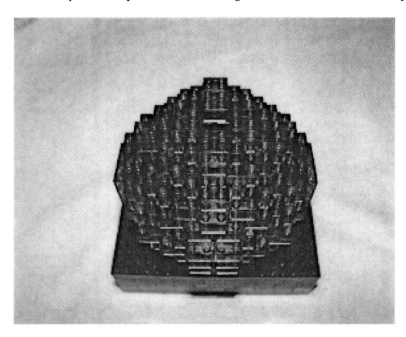

Figure 4-24. *The second-to-last layer of the sphere*

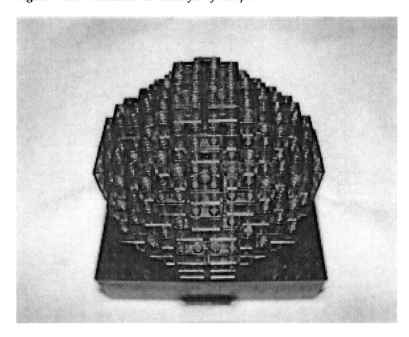

Figure 4-25. *The sphere is completed with a 4 × 4 stud layer*

Figure 4-26. *The completed crystal ball*

With the crystal ball completed, you need something to trigger the RFID reader.

Building the Magic Wand

The glass capsule RFID tag is the size of a grain of rice and can fit into most LEGO openings. To go with the crystal ball, you will build a magic wand. The wand will consist of a 32M Technic Axle, round 2 x 2 bricks with cross axle holes in the middle, and a round 2 x 2 tile to hold the RFID tag in (see Figure 4-27).

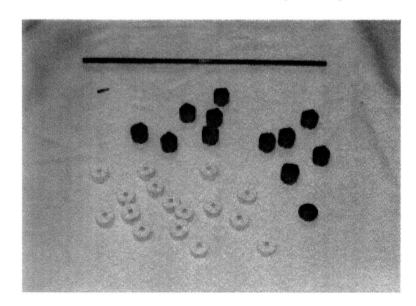

Figure 4-27. *The parts used to make the LEGO RFID wand*

The best way to start the wand is to put a couple of the 2 x 2 round bricks together and cap the top with the 2 x 2 round tile. Then slide the Technic axle in so the RFID tag is secured tightly and does not rattle around when the wand is waved. Once the RFID tag is hidden in the LEGO bricks, the other round 2 x 2 bricks can be slid up the axle and firmly pushed together to create the wand. Once it is finished, like in Figure 4-28, it can be waved in front of the base to bring the crystal ball to life.

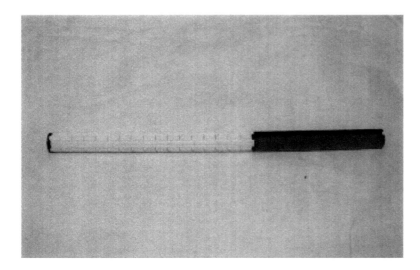

Figure 4-28. *The completed wand*

Summary

RFID is a technology that is becoming quite ubiquitous; it can be found in everyday life. Now you can utilize it to make your Arduino LEGO sculptures come to life. The tags can be used to trigger all sorts of actions and effects, and they can vary based on the different RFID tags that are waved in front of the RFID reader.

What else can you do with the RFID reader? What different effects can you make the RFID reader do based on different tags? Can you create different light patterns or colors based on RFID? Or can you add in some other features that different tags can trigger in it?

▓ ▓ ▓

CHAPTER 5

Animating the TARDIS

For 50 years now, the British Broadcasting Company has been airing Doctor Who. Since it relaunched in 2005, Doctor Who fandom has been steadily growing. The most iconic image of the program is the blue box that the Doctor travels in, known as the TARDIS, which stands for Time And Relative Dimension In Space. The TARDIS can take the Doctor to any time or place in the past, present, or future. You will take it into the realm of LEGO.

The TARDIS you will build cannot travel through space or time, nor is it larger on the inside. It will, however, be able to light up like the TARDIS does on the show, and it will be able to make the iconic TARDIS sounds. The look is based on the TARDIS of the tenth Doctor, played by David Tennant. There are minor variations between the different looks of the TARDIS for the different Doctors, but with minor adjustments it can be made to look like the TARDIS of other Doctors.

The TARDIS will be built using Studs Not On Top techniques, so that it doesn't look like it is built from LEGO bricks (in other words, you will be hiding the studs). Then you will use the Arduino to bring it to life. The Arduino will allow it to have lights and sounds just like the TARDIS on the television program.

A list of the parts in this chapter can be found in the appendix.

Doctoring the TARDIS

The first step is to have a way for the TARDIS to be able to make sounds, which is not inherently built into the Arduino. To do so, you will be using a Wave Shield from Adafruit Industries (see Figure 5-1). The Wave Shield allows the Arduino to play WAV files through a speaker or headphones and gives the ability to play music, sound effects, or any other audio that can be digitized for listening. Like the Motor Shield, the first step is to assemble the shield (see Figure 5-2). The full directions to do so can be found on the Adafruit web site at www.ladyada.net/make/waveshield/make.html.

Figure 5-1. *The unassembled Wave Shield*

Figure 5-2. *The assembled Wave Shield*

Once all the soldering is done and the Wave Shield is built, the sounds need to be added. This requires an SD memory card, which can be found at any electronics or camera store, many drugstores, and other large retailers; they can also be ordered online. The sounds for the TARDIS and Doctor Who can be found online with a little searching, but are mostly found in MP3 format. They will need to be converted to a WAV format to make them compatible. This can be done in iTunes or using free software, but take care to specify the 44KHz WAV formatted audio file in order for it to be able to be played by the Wave Shield. An online converter can be found at http://media.io/.

There are two ways to hear the output from the Wave Shield. The port on the lower left of Figure 5-2 is a headphone port, and a pair of headphones or speakers can be plugged in to it. The alternative is to solder a speaker into the two holes behind the headphone port. In this chapter, you will be soldering in a speaker (as seen in Figure 5-3), but to get louder sound, a powered speaker can be plugged in instead.

Figure 5-3. Wave Shield with speaker soldered in

Coding the Wave Shield

With the Wave Shield assembled to use with the Arduino, the next step is to upload some code to the Arduino. Listing 5-1 contains the code for the TARDIS, which is based on code to play WAVs by LadyAda. The Arduino and Wave Shield will play the sounds that are stored in the SD card and light the top of the TARDIS, then go dark and silent for a preset amount of time.

Listing 5-1. Playing the Music and Lighting the TARDIS

```
#include "WaveHC.h"
#include "WaveUtil.h"


SdReader card;    // This object holds the information for the card
FatVolume vol;    // This holds the information for the partition on the card
```

```
FatReader root;   // This holds the information for the volumes root directory
WaveHC wave;      // This is the only wave (audio) object, since we will only play one at a time

uint8_t dirLevel; // indent level for file/dir names    (for prettyprinting)
dir_t dirBuf;     // buffer for directory reads

//LED Variables
int ledvalue = 0;                          // variable to keep the actual value
int ledpin = 6;                            // light connected to digital pin 6
int up=1;
int delaytime;

/*
 * Define macro to put error messages in flash memory
 */
#define error(msg) error_P(PSTR(msg))

// Function definitions (we define them here, but the code is below)
void play(FatReader &dir);

///////////////////////////////////// SETUP
void setup() {
  Serial.begin(9600);                      // set up Serial library at 9600 bps for debugging
  pinMode(6, OUTPUT);
  pinMode(17, OUTPUT);

  putstring_nl("\nWave test!");            // say we woke up!

  putstring("Free RAM: ");                 // This can help with debugging, running out of RAM is bad
  Serial.println(FreeRam());

  //  if (!card.init(true)) {              //play with 4 MHz spi if 8MHz isn't working for you
  if (!card.init()) {                      //play with 8 MHz spi (default faster!)
    error("Card init. failed!");           // Something went wrong, lets print out why
  }

  // enable optimize read - some cards may timeout. Disable if you're having problems
  card.partialBlockRead(true);

  // Now we will look for a FAT partition!
  uint8_t part;
  for (part = 0; part < 5; part++) {       // we have up to 5 slots to look in
    if (vol.init(card, part))
      break;                               // we found one, let's bail
  }
  if (part == 5) {                         // if we ended up not finding one  :(
    error("No valid FAT partition!");      // Something went wrong, lets print out why
  }

  // Lets tell the user about what we found
  putstring("Using partition ");
  Serial.print(part, DEC);
```

```
  putstring(", type is FAT");
  Serial.println(vol.fatType(),DEC);      // FAT16 or FAT32?

  // Try to open the root directory
  if (!root.openRoot(vol)) {
    error("Can't open root dir!");        // Something went wrong,
  }

  // Whew! We got past the tough parts.
  putstring_nl("Files found (* = fragmented):");

  // Print out all of the files in all the directories.
  root.ls(LS_R | LS_FLAG_FRAGMENTED);

}

/////////////////////////////////// LOOP
void loop() {

  delay(500);
  root.rewind();
  play(root);
 ledvalue=0;
analogWrite(ledpin, ledvalue);

  delayTime=7 * 60 * 1000; //7 minutes * 60 seconds * 1000 milliseconds = 420000
  delay(delayTime);
  Serial.println("loopit");
}

/////////////////////////////////// HELPERS
/*
 * print error message and halt
 */
void error_P(const char *str) {
  PgmPrint("Error: ");
  SerialPrint_P(str);
  sdErrorCheck();
  while(1);
}
/*
 * print error message and halt if SD I/O error, great for debugging!
 */
void sdErrorCheck(void) {
  if (!card.errorCode()) return;
  PgmPrint("\r\nSD I/O error: ");
  Serial.print(card.errorCode(), HEX);
  PgmPrint(", ");
  Serial.println(card.errorData(), HEX);
  while(1);
}
```

```
/*
 * play recursively - possible stack overflow if subdirectories too nested
 */
void play(FatReader &dir) {

  FatReader file;
  while (dir.readDir(dirBuf) > 0) {          // Read every file in the directory one at a time

    // Skip it if not a subdirectory and not a WAV file
    if (!DIR_IS_SUBDIR(dirBuf)
        && strncmp_P((char *)&dirBuf.name[8], PSTR("WAV"), 3)) {
      continue;
    }

    Serial.println();                        // clear out a new line

    for (uint8_t i = 0; i < dirLevel; i++) {
      Serial.print(' ');                     // this is for prettyprinting, put spaces in front
    }
    if (!file.open(vol, dirBuf)) {           // open the file in the directory
      error("file.open failed");             // something went wrong
    }

    if (file.isDir()) {                      // check if we opened a new directory
      putstring("Subdir: ");
      printEntryName(dirBuf);
      dirLevel += 2;                         // add more spaces
      // play files in subdirectory
      play(file);                            // recursive!
      dirLevel -= 2;
    } else {
      // Aha! we found a file that isn't a directory
      putstring("Playing ");
      printEntryName(dirBuf);                // print it out
      if (!wave.create(file)) {              // Figure out, is it a WAV proper?
        putstring(" Not a valid WAV");       // ok skip it
      } else {
        Serial.println();                    // Hooray it IS a WAV proper!
        wave.play();                         // make some noise!

        uint8_t n = 0;
        while (wave.isplaying) {             // playing occurs in interrupts, so we print dots in realtime
          if (up == 1) {
            ledvalue=ledvalue+3;             //Gradually increase the illumination if we are lighting up
          } else {
            ledvalue=ledvalue-3;             //Otherwise decrease to lower the lighting
          }

          if (ledvalue > 255) {              //If we reach maximum illumination, start decreasing
            up=0;
            ledvalue=ledvalue-3;
          } else if (ledvalue < 0) {         //Otherwise we're going to make the light brighter
```

116

```
            up=1;
            ledvalue=ledvalue+3;
          }
        analogWrite(ledpin, ledvalue);

        putstring(".");
        if (!(++n % 32)) Serial.println();
        delay(100);

      }
      sdErrorCheck();                                  // everything OK?
      // if (wave.errors)Serial.println(wave.errors);  // wave decoding errors
    }
  }
}
}
```

It is worth noting that this code will not work without downloading the latest version of the Wave Shield drivers. Since they did not come with the Arduino software, they must be downloaded from the software repository at http://code.google.com/p/wavehc/. Download the file and unzip it. From there, copy the WaveHC folder into the Arduino Libraries folder. The location of the folder can be found in the Arduino preferences. If the Arduino software is open at the time, you must quit and restart the Arduino software so it can read the new library and use it to compile.

In the setup() function, you start by testing how much RAM is free to make sure it is available, since the Wave Shield is more system intensive than prior programs. Although the software does not make use of this information, you print it to the serial monitor for debugging purposes. The next step is to make sure that the SD card is readable. If the SD card is formatted properly in a FAT format (most SD cards are preformatted in a FAT32 file system) and the card is securely in the slot, then there is probably a bad solder joint somewhere. Since the solder joints are fairly close together on the board, check the pins fastened to the SD card holder as well as the wires in the lower left that lead from the WAV playing holes to the Arduino pin holes.

If the card can be read, the setup() function optimizes the ability to read, then checks if there is a valid FAT partition on the drive. Since there are multiple parts of the card that can hold the FAT partition, it checks each in turn, and once it finds one, it will make sure it can read the root directory in the partition. If all of those different things check out, it reads through the directories on the card and pulls out the names of the different files on the card in order to play them during the execution of the loop() function.

The loop() function is where you play the music. The loop() simply rewinds the WAV file back to the beginning, then plays the music and/or sound effects that are stored on the SD card. Since the LED on top of the TARDIS is running as part of the playing of the sounds, you do an analogWrite to turn off the light, regardless of where in the cycle the light may be, then wait the delaytime value before playing again. While delaytime is 7 minutes (7 minutes times 60 seconds times 1000 milliseconds), it can easily be changed to shorten the time between executions.

The main work of the code is done in the play() function. The play() function recursively traverses the directories on the SD card, seeking out the subdirectories and will play every WAV file it finds as it goes through. It is not necessary to put the WAV files in directories beyond the root directory, but if they are put into directories, this code will traverse the directory structure and seek them out. When it finds a file, it opens the file and checks if it is a WAV. If it is a WAV file, it calls the wave.play() function and starts playing the file. You create a loop with the while (wave.isplaying), and it will stay in this loop until the end of the sound. In here, you are raising and lowering the LED, but you can't do it in a for loop, like you did with the crystal ball so that it is controlled by the while loop. Instead you set a variable called up, and you raise the value of the analogWrite with each iteration until it reaches 255 (the maximum value) and flips the flag to start decrementing until it hits zero. When the loop ends, the value of the LED is left where it is, to be reset when the play() function ends, and it returns to the loop() function. You are also printing periods to the serial monitor so that you can see if the file is playing for debugging purposes.

The Chameleon Circuit: Building the TARDIS

Now that you have working code to play sound effects and light up the top of the TARDIS, it is time to actually build it. While the first layer is plates, like in previous projects, you will not be building a three-plate base. Instead you will use plates to secure bricks for the base. Figure 5-4 shows the 22 x 22 stud base.

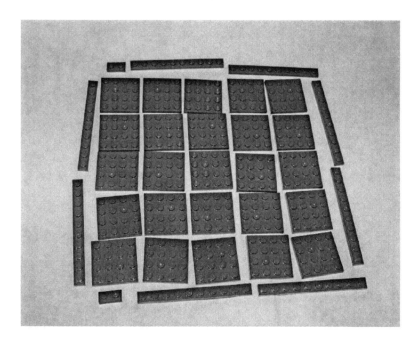

Figure 5-4. *The 22 ×22 stud layout of plates*

The plates in Figure 5-4 are spread out to make them easier to see, but the next step is to push them together and secure them with blue bricks. The bricks should cover the seams of the plates and hold them in place. Notice the 1 x 4 groove in the upper right corner of Figure 5-5. This is where you will lay the power cable for the Arduino, so that it can be integrated into your design smoothly.

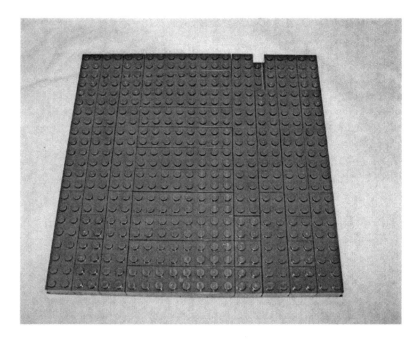

Figure 5-5. *A layer of bricks laid onto the plates*

The two layers of plates and bricks will be firm, but will be made stronger with a layer of tiles. The TARDIS should have no visible studs, so you need to cover all of the studs in the middle and the edges with tiles to give it a smooth appearance. The side with the doors will also be covered with tiles so that they can slide smoothly over the base. The locations of the walls will have a plate fill in the groove that the walls can be laid upon. The groove that the power cable is laid in will not be covered by plates, but tiles will be laid down in their appropriate places (see Figure 5-6).

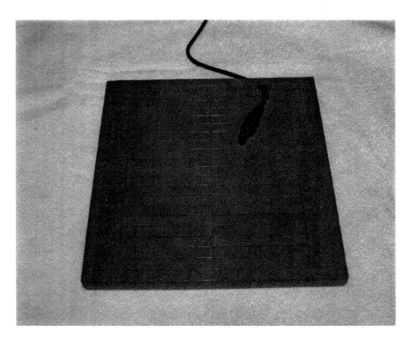

Figure 5-6. *A layer of tiles and plates is laid down on top of the bricks to hide the studs*

Building the Walls

Now that the base is done, it's time to start building the walls. Since the TARDIS design features very defined seams, you will be laying everything down to preserve them but still build a strong structure. You are laying down another layer of plates above the base, but the corners should be 2 x 2 studs and two 2 x 8 plates between them (see Figure 5-7). You are also laying down two 2 x 8 plates in the front, even though they will not be connected to the base, so that the doors will have the same layout as you build them up. There will also be a one-stud hole to allow the power cord through. This will give the cord enough room to be firmly entrenched in the base but have room to move, and the plate to the outer edge of the layer will hide the cable hole from the outside.

Figure 5-7. *Plates are put down over the plates on the base*

You have a firm base to build upon, so you can now put down bricks. The bricks are going to follow the same pattern as the plates in Figure 5-7. In Figure 5-8, the 2 x 8 plates are covered with 2 x 8 bricks and the corners are covered with 2 x 2 bricks. Don't worry about the seams not being covered; you'll take care of that soon.

Figure 5-8. *Bricks are laid down on top of the plates*

The panels of the TARDIS walls start to become defined as you start to raise them. The edges of the 2 x 8 bricks each receive a 1 x 2 brick, except for the ones in the front corners. The doors each receive a 2 x 2 hinge to connect them to the corner next to them; those corners each receive a 1 x 2 brick to fill them out, and the perpendicular side gets a 1 x 1 brick to give the hinge room to move when opening the doors inwards. Each of the 2 x 8 bricks has six 1 x 2 jumper plates between the 1 x 2. The panels on the TARDIS are receded, but going one stud back would be too much, so you will use jumpers to push the panel halfway back, giving it the proper look and feel (see Figure 5-9).

Figure 5-9. *Jumpers, hinges, and 1 x 2 bricks are laid out*

Three LEGO plates are the same height as one brick. You laid out the jumpers (shown in Figure 5-9) and will do so again at the top of the panel, which means a third plate will be needed to give the panels their proper height. In Figure 5-10, eight 1 x 6 plates are placed on top of the jumpers to adjust the height to the necessary size to fill out the panels.

Figure 5-10. *1 × 6 plates are put on top of the jumper plates*

The walls start to gain height as the hinges are secured with 2 x 2 bricks, as are the other corners. The 1 x 2 bricks, including the hinges and the 1 x 1 bricks, are covered with another 1 x 2 brick. The 1 x 6 plates are then covered by 1 x 6 bricks; see Figure 5-11 for reference.

Figure 5-11. *1 × 6 bricks go on top of the 1 × 6 plates and the other bricks stack one higher*

Once you have a firm base and the beginnings of the walls, you can begin to secure them.

Securing the Walls

Since you are keeping the visible seams based on the TARDIS from the TV show, you will use a little trickery to make it seem like the panels and corners are independent while they are actually secured in the back. On the four corners, you will put 2 x 2 brick corners, which are 2 x 2 bricks with one stud missing. The left and the right walls will have 1 x 2 bricks go from on top of the 1 x 2 bricks to the corners, and 1 x 1 bricks will go in front of them to make it seem the same. With the two panels next to each other, you will put a 1 x 2 across the two 1 x 2 bricks and put two 1 x 1 bricks in front of them. The two side walls will now be secured to the corners and to each other, as seen in Figure 5-12. Additionally, you will place another 1 x 6 brick on top of the stacks of 1 x 6 bricks.

Figure 5-12. *The two side walls are anchored to the corners and to each other*

With the two sides secure, it's now time to do the same to the back wall. Spread 1 x 2 bricks from the edges of the panels to the corners and across the two panels next to each other to fortify the back wall and hold it in place as well. The side panels and other two corners will be stacked with 1 x 2 and 2 x 2 bricks to bring them up one more level. The 1 x 6 bricks will also be raised one more level (see Figure 5-13).

Figure 5-13. *The back wall is secured in place and the rest of the bricks are raised a level*

Now the 1 x 6 bricks are slightly lower than the other bricks, so you need to put down plates to make it even. You are laying down 1 x 2 jumper plates on top of the 1 x 6 bricks so that they will be even in height and can hold the bricks that will be stacked on top of them (see Figure 5-14).

Figure 5-14. *1 ×2 jumper plates are placed on top of the 1 ×6 bricks*

The first set of panels is completed by placing a 2 x 8 brick across the 1 x 2 jumper plates. The jumpers will line up with the holes in the bottom of the 2 x 8 brick, so it will securely hold the panels together. This will not only be the top for this set of panels, but will be the bottom for the next set as well. The corners will be raised to the same level as the 2 x 8 bricks with 2 x 2 bricks (see Figure 5-15).

Figure 5-15. *The first set of panels is completed with 2 × 8 bricks*

The TARDIS itself has three sets of panels with windows on top, as well as the two doors, so you need to do the same. You are going to copy the process two more times to get three sets of panels, including securing each of them to the corners and the panels next to them. Figures 5-16 and 5-17 show the second and third sets of panels being raised.

Figure 5-16. *The second set of panels is raised*

Figure 5-17. *The third set of panels is added*

Since you don't want to have any studs showing, you need to use a Studs Not On Top (SNOT) technique. SNOT techniques tend to use bricks in unusual ways in order to hide the studs. You're going to use one such technique in order to create your windows.

Building the Windows

The way the windows are framed in the TARDIS, you need to be able to put plates and/or tiles between bricks to get the proper effect. Since there needs to be a horizontal frame in addition to the vertical ones, you need to build the windows in two ways. The first is a simple stack of blue plates and white bricks capped by a blue tile. In Figure 5-18, the parts used are on the left and the assembled one is on the right. You need to make eight of these.

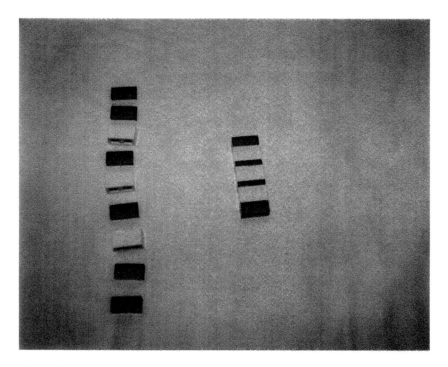

Figure 5-18. *The windows are made from a stack of plates and bricks. The parts are on the left and the assembled windows are on the right*

For the second set of windows, which you build in Figure 5-19, the middle white 1 x 2 brick is replaced by a 1 x 1 white brick and a 1 x 1 white Technic brick, which will hold a ½ Technic pin, with a 1 x 6 tile attaching to it. The center stud beneath the 1 x 6 tile will go over the ½ pin and should cover the length of your windows. Again, you need eight of these.

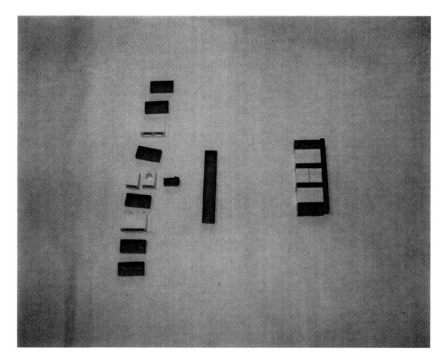

Figure 5-19. *The other eight windows will be constructed like this one*

Now that you have the windows, you need to prepare the TARDIS for them.

Installing the Windows

You will start this level the same way that you started the previous panel sets, but instead of jumper plates, you will just put in tiles to keep the smooth, studless appearance. The two sides are secured to the corners here to keep building strong, as seen in Figure 5-20.

Figure 5-20. *The next set of panels prepares for the windows*

The windows that you built will be put in sideways, which means that they need something to attach to. The outer 1 x 2 bricks (the ones closest to the corners) will all be 1 x 2 Technic bricks with ½ Technic pins inserted into them. This will give a stud for the windows to attach to, as shown in Figure 5-21.

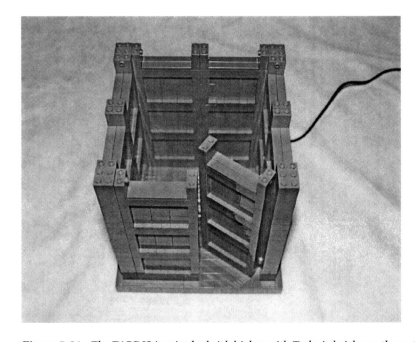

Figure 5-21. *The TARDIS is raised a brick higher with Technic bricks on the outer edges*

The windows with the 1 x 6 tile on the side will be attached first. The tile edge should be up, and the higher of the two stud holes will be put on the Technic pins. The windows will not be entirely secure yet, but they will hold in place for the remainder of the building of this section. As you install the windows, you will raise the sides a level higher as well. You will secure the back wall of the TARDIS and secure each set of panels to the one next to it to strengthen the structure for the last time (see Figure 5-22).

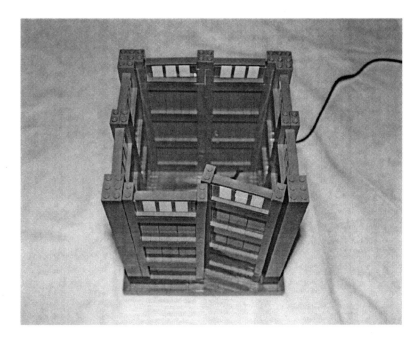

Figure 5-22. *The first set of windows is attached*

By adding another 1 x 2 Technic brick to the inner 1 x 2 brick stack, you add a place for the other window set. This is also the last level before you lock everything into place with another 2 x 8 brick, so this is where you will add another set of hinges for the doors. Like the first time, the hinges go from the 2 x 2 pillars to the outer edges of the walls, with a 1 x 2 brick complimenting them on the pillar, and a 1 x 1 brick atop the 1 x 2 bricks on the perpendicular edges to give the hinges room to open (Figure 5-23).

Figure 5-23. *The second set of 1 ×2 Technic bricks is added to hold the second set of windows, as well as the second set of hinges*

The second set of windows goes in the same way as the first set. The windows will be on their side with the ½ pin going into the higher of the two peg holes. Again, it will not be completely secure, but the following step will lock it into place (see Figure 5-24).

Figure 5-24. *The second set of windows is added*

With the windows installed, they need to be locked into place. Like the previous sets of panels, you need to put a 2 x 8 on top of each of the sets of windows and a 2 x 2 brick on top of each of those pillars. Figure 5-25 shows the final bricks for the TARDIS body.

Figure 5-25. *The final set of bricks for the panels is added*

For the doors to move smoothly, they need to have tiles on top; otherwise they will stick on the door frame. Figure 5-26 shows the tiles added to the tops of the doors and the plates placed on top of the other bricks to keep a consistent height across the entire body of the TARDIS.

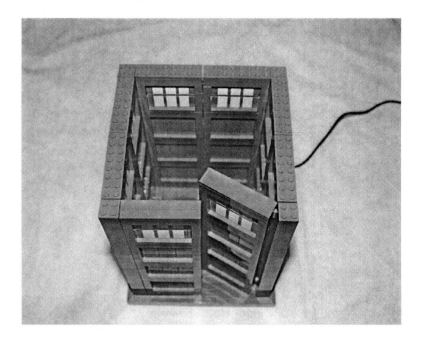

Figure 5-26. *Tiles are added to make the door move smoothly and plates are added for consistent height*

Now you need to add a level of brick, but you want to be able to hang the "Police Box" sign off the side. So instead of putting down a level of bricks, you'll do three levels of plates. The first level will not support all of the plates because you have an opening in the front, but you can hold it in place by letting it rest on top of the doors until the second level. On the third level, you will lay down a 1 x 2 - 1 x 4 bracket. This piece has a 1 x 2 stud plate on top and a 1 x 4 plate at a 90 degree angle, allowing it to hang pieces off the side. Figures 5-27 through 5-29 show the building of the stack of plates.

Figure 5-27. *The first layer of plates is laid down. Portions of the front plates are resting on the doors and are not secured yet*

Figure 5-28. *The second layer of plates is laid down, covering the seams to lock the plates into place*

Figure 5-29. *The third layer has a 1 × 2 - 1 × 4 bracket at the middle of each side*

Now you want to hide the studs on the top as well as add a place to put the sign. The outer studs of that level will be covered with tiles so they will not be seen as you continue to build upwards. Two 1 x 8 tiles will be added to each of the 1 x 4 plates on the bracket, giving you a place to put the signs when you are ready for them (see Figure 5-30).

Figure 5-30. *Tiles are placed around the edge and on the sides*

Adding the Arduino

Before you continue to build up, now is a good time to place the Arduino. We didn't build a place for the Arduino into the design of the TARDIS since we have limited room (and our version is not bigger on the inside). Instead, you are going to use Velcro to hold the Arduino inside the TARDIS. In Figure 5-31, the Arduino with Wave Shield can be seen with the Velcro, and in Figure 5-32, the Velcro is applied and the unit is adhered within what you have built so far.

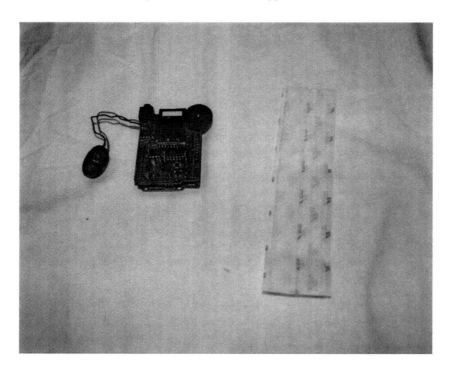

Figure 5-31. *The Arduino setup and the Velcro*

Figure 5-32. *The Velcro is applied to the back of the Arduino and speaker, and that unit is adhered to the back of the TARDIS. A layer of 2 ×2 bricks is placed in a ring on the exposed studs*

With the additional 2 x 2 bricks placed around the top of the TARDIS, tiles need to be placed around the edge. Figure 5-33 shows the tiles placed atop the bricks.

Figure 5-33. *With the additional 2 ×2 bricks placed around the top of the TARDIS, tiles are to be placed around the edge*

Now that the Arduino is inside the TARDIS, you can continue to build up the top.

Back to the Body . . .

The body will have a cookie jar type top, so this is the last level for the body. A set of bricks two studs wide will be placed on top of the current level and then secured by covering the entire level with tiles, so the lip can easily rest on top (see Figures 5-34 and 5-35).

Figure 5-34. *The last set of bricks for the body is placed on top*

Figure 5-35. *The top level is covered in tiles*

The last step to complete the body is to create labels for it.

Creating Labels

The labels consist of four Police Box banners for the top and a single sign for the left door. The best labels are waterslide decals, but if they are unavailable, paper labels from any stationary store can be used; just be sure to get the 8" x 10" sheets so that the labels are not cut in the middle. Figure 5-36 shows what the labels should look like, and Figure 5-37 shows the completed TARDIS body with labels applied.

PUBLIC TELEPHONE
FREE
FOR USE OF
PUBLIC
ADVICE & ASSISTANCE
OBTAINABLE IMMEDIATELY
OFFICER & CALL
RESPOND TO ALL CALLS
PULL TO OPEN

Figure 5-36. *The decals for the Police Box banner and TARDIS doordecal*

Figure 5-37. *The completed TARDIS body*

Now that the body is done, you need to give your TARDIS a roof.

Building the Roof

Since you are going with a cookie jar type top, it needs an edge to hold it in place when it slides into the body, and to give the slopes something to sit on. In Figure 5-38, you start with a ring of bricks. The ring will fit in the opening on top of the TARDIS body.

Figure 5-38. *The initial ring for the TARDIS lid*

The second layer of the lid will have 2 x 3 33 1/3 slopes around the edge, as well as the 2 x 2 33 1/3 slope corners. Since this will not make for a very strong foundation, the inner ring of studs will be filled in with a two-stud ring of bricks, as seen in Figure 5-39.

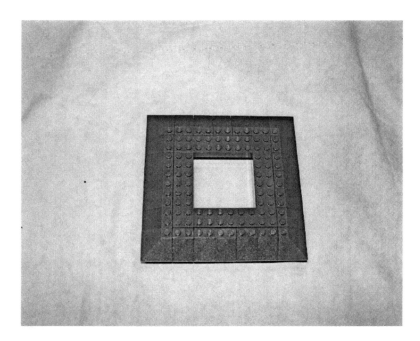

Figure 5-39. *A ring of slopes is laid down and is supported by an inner ring of bricks*

You now need to lay down two more levels of slopes. This first level, as seen in Figure 5-40, sits on top of the exposed studs of the layer in Figure 5-39. It is secured by locking in on the level beneath it, but the level above it, which is seen in Figure 5-41, has the slopes' outer studs attach to the slopes beneath it. While not completely secure, they will hold in place well enough for you to work with.

Figure 5-40. *The slopes completely cover the studs beneath them*

Figure 5-41. *The last layer of slopes have their outer edge on the slopes beneath them*

Now you will flip over the lid and secure the top layer of slopes in place. The center piece securing the slopes in place is a 2 x 4 plate with holes in it. You are using a Technic plate so you can feed an LED through the hole and have the top of the TARDIS light up. The 2 x 4 is surrounded by a ring of plates to lock the plates more firmly and cover the seams (Figure 5-42).

Figure 5-42. *An LED is run through the hole in the middle of the 2 × 4 plate and more plates secure the slopes*

When you flip the lid back over, you push the LED over one of the studs and push a 2 x 2 corner piece into the hole. There will be enough room to slide the LED leads into the hole after the 2 x 2 corner is inserted, so push the LED down so that it does not stick out higher than the brick and so that the two leads do not touch (see Figure 5-43).

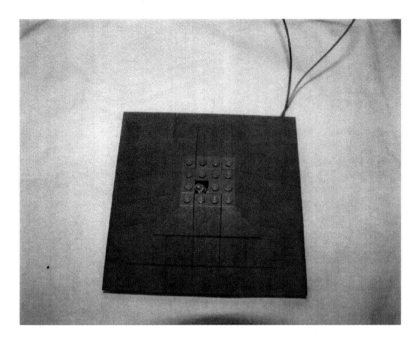

Figure 5-43. *The 2 ×2 corner piece with the white LED in the corner*

The studs are still exposed on top, so a ring of 1 x 3 tiles covers the outer exposed studs. A round 2 x 2 clear brick is placed on top of the corner brick in the middle, which can be seen in Figure 5-44. A second 2 x 2 clear round is placed on top of the first with a 2 x 2 round tile on top; this completes the TARDIS, as shown in Figure 5-45. Even though the LED is hidden beneath the round, the clear bricks will refract the light and the light will be seen clearly when the music and sounds start to play (see Figure 5-46).

Figure 5-44. *Tiles are placed around the top of the slopes, and a clear 2 × 2 round is placed over the 2 × 2 corner*

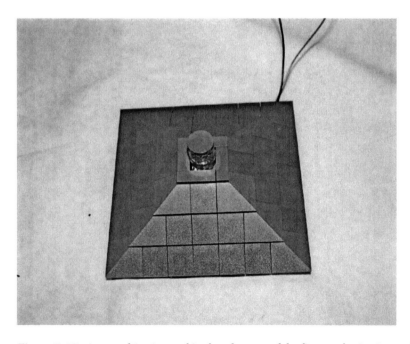

Figure 5-45. *A second 2 × 2 round is placed on top of the first, and a 2 × 2 round tile is placed on top*

Figure 5-46. *The LED is attached to the ground and pin 6, the lid is placed onto the top of the body, and the TARDIS is completed*

Summary

Doctor Who fandom is at an all-time high, so you used SNOT techniques to build your own TARDIS. You were able to capture the look and feel without having any exposed studs. Although it cannot travel through space and time, nor does it fade out when it activates, it can simulate the lights and sounds of the TARDIS that occur when the Doctor travels.

What else can you make the TARDIS do? Can you build a sonic screwdriver that will trigger the TARDIS? Can you make it play different sounds based on different triggers? Can you use the TARDIS to battle intergalactic machinations of alien overlords?

CHAPTER 6

■ ■ ■

Controlling LEGO Trains with Arduino

The LEGO Group has its own mechanical system, the Power Functions system. Power Functions are a system of motors and lights that are made by LEGO and are used to power and control such projects as dinosaurs, bulldozers and trucks. There is also a thriving train community that uses LEGO trains to create large, ornate multi-train layouts that run through LEGO cities and towns crowded with buildings and people as they go about their LEGO lives. Like the other Power Functions creations, the trains are controlled remotely to tell each train which direction and how fast to travel.

The LEGO Power Functions are predominantly controlled by remote controls that use infrared technology. IR is commonly used in devices like TV remote controls to send signals to devices and react to them. The Arduino can both send and receive IR signals with the proper connections. A simple infrared LED and the proper frequencies can be used to mimic these signals and control these devices.

For this project, you will take an Arduino and use it to control a LEGO train. The Arduino can control all the same functions as the Power Functions remote, but it should be more reliable and send a cleaner signal to the IR receiver in the train to allow for finer control of the train. While the Arduino can control up to eight trains, you will be working with just one for this project.

A list of the parts in this chapter can be found in the appendix.

Arduino Train Controls

The most basic things you need for this project are an Arduino and an infrared LED, but that wouldn't give you enough control over the train, so you will add a potentiometer, a button, and some LEDs to be able to control the train and have some visible reactions. Figure 6-1 shows a diagram of the wiring and Figure 6-2 shows the required hardware on a breadboard.

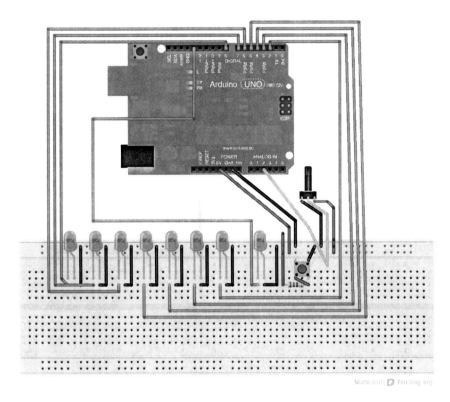

Figure 6-1. *Diagram of the wiring for the train controller*

Figure 6-2. *The Arduino hardware for the train project*

The component in the upper right is a type of a variable resistor called a potentiometer. As the shaft turns, the resistance increases or decreases. Using one of the Arduino's analog inputs, it is possible to read this value and do something in your code like control the brightness of an LED or, in this case, the speed of the train. There are three connections coming from it: far left is ground, middle connects to a pin, and far right connects to the 5V pin. The middle connection has to go to an Analog In pin because unlike a button, which has an on state and an off state, the potentiometer returns a numeric value from 0 to 1024, similar to the way you used the Analog Out pins to send values of 0 to 255 to dim LEDs. You are going to use the potentiometer to control the speed of the train.

The button next to the potentiometer is a Normally Open (NO) push button. Normally Open means that there is no connection when the button is not being pressed. Pressing the button creates a connection and the Arduino receives a signal to let it know that the circuit has been closed. On the breadboard between the Arduino and the button is a 200 Ohm resistor. The resistor's job is to provide the path of least resistance for the flow of the electricity, so the Arduino doesn't think the button was pushed when it wasn't.

The LEDs are going to display the current speed of the train as it is running. Since Power Functions have eight speeds (stop and one to seven), the LEDs will be lit up to display the current speed. The LEDs will be connected to pins 2 through 8 on the Arduino and are connected on the breadboard to the ground. The infrared LED will be used to send the signal to the train and is connected like a normal LED, in pin 13.

Programming the Train Controls

With the hardware set up, the next step is to get the code ready. The Arduino sketch in shown in Listing 6-1.

Listing 6-1. Train Control Code

```
#include <legopowerfunctions.h>

int fwdSpeed[] = {PWM_FLT, PWM_FWD1, PWM_FWD2,
    PWM_FWD3, PWM_FWD4, PWM_FWD5, PWM_FWD6, PWM_FWD7};
int revSpeed[] = {PWM_FLT, PWM_REV1, PWM_REV2,
    PWM_REV3, PWM_REV4, PWM_REV5, PWM_REV6, PWM_REV7};
int curSpeed = 0;

// IR led on port 13
LEGOPowerFunctions lego(13);
int potPin = A2;     // select the input pin for the potentiometer
int val = 0;
int setSpeed = 0;
int ledPin[] = {2, 3, 4, 5, 6, 7, 8};
int buttonPin = 10;
int buttonState=0;
int fwdRev=0;

void setup() {
  for (int i=0; i<7; i++) {
    pinMode(ledPin[i], OUTPUT);
  }
  Serial.begin(9600);
  pinMode(buttonPin, INPUT);
}
```

```
void loop() {
  val = analogRead(potPin);                    // read the value from the sensor
  Serial.print("POT: ");
  Serial.println(val);

  buttonState = digitalRead(buttonPin);
  Serial.print("BUTTON: ");
  Serial.println(buttonState);

if (buttonState) fwdRev = !fwdRev;

setSpeed=val/125;
  if(setSpeed>7) setSpeed=7;

  for (int i=0; i<7; i++) {
      digitalWrite(ledPin[i], LOW);
  }

  for (i=0; i<setSpeed; i++) {
    digitalWrite(ledPin[i], HIGH);
  }

  Serial.print("SPEED: ");
  Serial.println(setSpeed);
  if (fwdRev==0) {
    curSpeed=fwdSpeed[setSpeed];
  } else {
    curSpeed=revSpeed[setSpeed];
  }
  lego.ComboPWM(curSpeed, curSpeed, CH1); // set speed
  delay(100);


}
```

The first thing the train needs is the LEGO Power Functions library for Arduino. This library makes it simple to interface with the infrared LED and make it talk to the train. You can find the library at http://arduino.cc/forum/index.php?topic=89310.0, where it can be downloaded, uncompressed and copied to the library folder. Restarting the Arduino software after it is installed will make the library accessible.

Once you have access to the library, you can set up arrays to hold the different speeds. You have two arrays, from zero to seven (stopped to top speed). One array is for going forward while the other array is for going in reverse. The curSpeed variable is passed to the movement function, and the fwdRev variable controls which direction the train travels.

The setup() function is just used to do some basic preparation for the loop() function. It does some initial definition of pins and opens the connection so that you can use the serial monitor for debugging purposes.

The loop() function starts by checking the values of the potentiometer and the button. If the button is pushed, it flips the value of the fwdRev variable. A 0 value will tell the train to go forward and a 1 value will tell the train to go in reverse. Then you look at the potentiometer. The potentiometer value goes from 0 to approximately 1024 and you divide by 7. Should the value be over 7, you set it to 7 to keep the speed within the accepted values and tell the train to crank up the speed.

Once you know the speed value, you can turn on that number of LEDs. You use a for loop with an array to turn all the lights off first, then turn on the same number of lights as the speed value. An if statement based on fwdRev tells the code whether to use the forward or reverse array, then sets that value to the curSpeed variable. That variable is then passed to the Power Functions function.

Power Functions have four channels and can be defined as red or blue, allowing for up to eight controls from one unit. The channel and the color are set on the IR receiver. Most LEGO remotes can control one channel at a time but have two switches or knobs to control red and blue simultaneously. The Arduino allows you to control more, even if you are not using it to its full capability in this project. The ComboPWM function (attached to the variable lego, defined right after the speed variables) has three variables passed to it: red speed, blue speed, and channel. For this program, you are making red and blue the same speed and only using channel 1, but it's easy to edit to add additional trains or do things with additional Power Functions motors.

Building the Train Station

With the code done, it's time to build the train station and then the train. First you will build the train control unit. You need someplace to put the Arduino and breadboard, so start with a stack of three plates again. Figure 6-3 shows the base.

Figure 6-3. *Three plates stacked for the base*

Place the Arduino and breadboard from Figure 6-2 on the base to build around them. You can use the breadboard in the base of the controller, but you may need to rearrange the layout. Lay out the Arduino and breadboard for spacing and build the first layer of the walls around it, as shown in Figure 6-4.

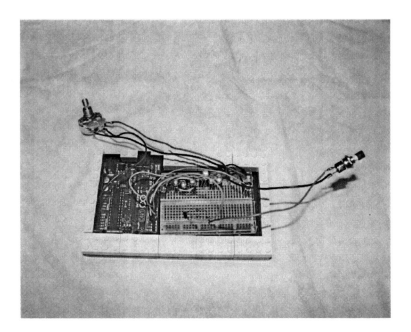

Figure 6-4. *The basic layout for the LEGO box to hold the Arduino and breadboard*

The box is built up and the parts inside are rearranged to fit in the box and to allow the LEDs to be seen from outside. The LED bulbs are pushed into 1 x 2 Technic bricks and the lights will shine out as the potentiometer is turned. Because the lights are recessed and covered, ultrabright LEDs are recommended so they can be viewed better. Figure 6-5 shows the second and third layers of the walls and the Technic bricks facing outwards from the front of the base.

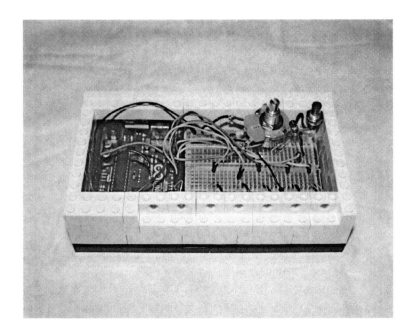

Figure 6-5. *The walls of the base are built up*

Figures 6-6 to 6-8 show the three layers of the lid being built up. Notice how the hole in the corner is left open for the IR LED, the potentiometer, and the button. While the hole is wide initially, it is made tighter on the second layer and finally covered as much as possible in the third layer.

Figure 6-6. *The first layer of the lid is laid down*

Figure 6-7. *The second layer of the lid*

Figure 6-8. The lid is completed, exposing the potentiometer, button, and IR LED in the back corner

This unit can be used as a handheld remote control for the train, either using batteries to have a more mobile experience or rooted to a limited space with a power cord. If it is going to remain in place, it is worth decorating the base to look like a train station or some train-related destination. Figure 6-9 shows some added flourishes so it doesn't look out of place next to the train tracks.

Figure 6-9. The base decorated to look like a train platform

Building a LEGO Train

There are three essential pieces for a LEGO train: the powered wheels, the battery box, and the IR receiver. The wheels connect to one of two plugs on the IR receiver, which defines it as either a red or a blue engine, and the IR receiver connects to a plug on the battery box. Figure 6-10 shows all three pieces.

Figure 6-10. *The powered wheels, battery box, and IR receiver*

Adding Wheels

First you need a base to connect everything to. Once you have the base (see Figure 6-11), you can flip it over and add the wheels (see Figure 6-12). The wheels on the back of the train will be powered, giving it a rear wheel drive, while the front wheels will be loose and just follow the tracks.

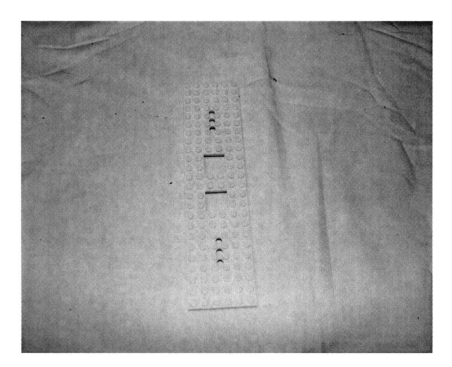

Figure 6-11. *The base for the train*

Figure 6-12. *The wheels are connected to the bottom and the cable from the back wheels is pushed through a hole*

With the wheels attached, you can flip over the base and set down the framework for the train (see Figure 6-13). You are building a basic train, but you can build any kind of train off this base. Your train's look is based on old steam locomotives, but it could be easily changed to a bullet train or tram.

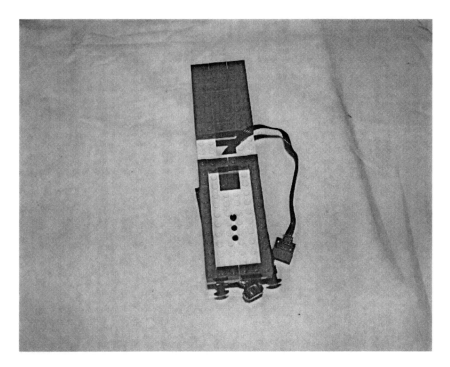

Figure 6-13.   *The framework for the train*

The front of the framework will be the locomotive, while the back will be the coal car, since it will be powering the train. For the second layer, though, just put down a second layer on top of the bricks you already laid down (Figure 6-14).

Figure 6-14. *The second layer of the train*

With two layers down, you can start to give it more shape. The third layer adds slopes to the front of the coal car and opens a groove for where the boiler's backhead would be located if it were an actual train. Otherwise, the front of the train gets another layer, as does the coal car (see Figure 6-15).

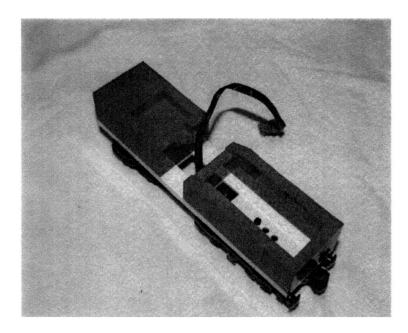

Figure 6-15. *The third layer starts to give the train shape*

The fourth layer gives the train more defined lines as you start to add more slopes. The front of the train has slopes that angle inwards and the control area is built up another brick high. The coal car takes another slope to angle it back further while a one-stud border goes around the rest of that area (see Figure 6-16).

Figure 6-16. *The train engine gets its curves, and the coal car gets its shape*

Adding the Battery Pack

Since your train is powered by battery instead of coal, you will put the battery pack in the coal car (see Figure 6-17). Once it is there, you can add the IR receiver and run the plugs from the wheels to the IR receiver to the battery pack. 1 x 2 red bricks are placed under the IR receiver to give it height for when you stack it on top of the battery pack. On the front, four stacks of three 1 x 1 bricks are placed at the corners of the control area and a stack of three 2 x 2 rounds are placed at the front of the train to simulate the smoke stack (see Figure 6-18).

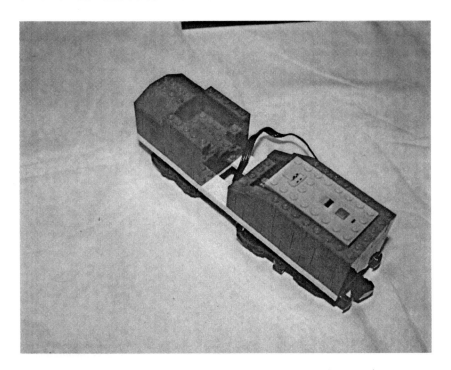

Figure 6-17. *The battery pack is placed in the coal car*

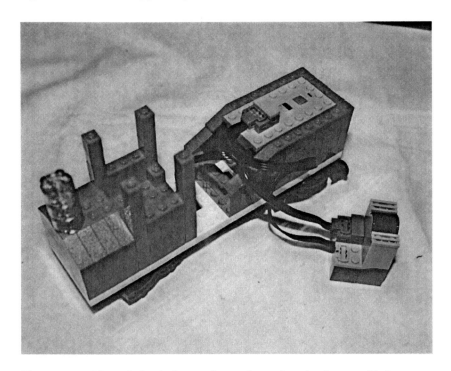

Figure 6-18. *The train is wired up as the smoke stack and poles are added*

Adding the IR Receiver

All that is left now is to place the IR receiver on top of the battery pack. Be sure not to cover the power button when adding the receiver; otherwise it will be hard to turn the train on and off. A roof and engineer are added to the front of the train (see Figure 6-19), and it is ready to pull into the station (see Figure 6-20).

Figure 6-19. *A roof and engineer are added to the front of the train while the IR receiver is added to the back*

Figure 6-20. *The train is ready to pull into the station*

Summary

The LEGO Group has a robust engine system and trains that can be made to be very interactive. With Arduino, they can be programmed to be far more complex than with the simple controls LEGO provides. Going further, adding sensors and input devices can make them even more interesting.

What kinds of things could you do to improve this system? Could you add sensors so the train interacts with the base when it approaches the station? Could you add an Ethernet shield and have an Internet-controlled train? Could you have multiple trains that can interact with each other and react as they go around the tracks?

■ ■ ■

CHAPTER 7

Building a Light-Sensitive Box

This project, which was inspired by a jewelry box. In the previous projects, you worked with servo motors, which predominantly have a limited field of motion of 180 degrees, but what happens if you want to make something turn all the way around, like the ornamentation in a jewelry box? This project will allow you to do so based on whether the box is open or closed.

Most jewelry boxes have a button hidden somewhere that controls the motor and tells the ornament to spin, but you will take a more technological approach to this concept. Instead, you will read how much light is in the box and based on that, you will tell the motor to spin.

A list of the parts in this chapter can be found in the appendix.

The Box's Mechanics

A photocell is a variable resistor that changes its resistance based on how much or how little light is hitting it. In this case, you are using a second resistor as a voltage divider, and it should be of equal value of the photocell. The photocell in the figures is rated at 10k, so you should use a 10k resistor. One pin from the photocell goes to the 5V pin to get current, while the other goes to both the Arduino pin and the resistor, the other pin of which goes to the ground. A diagram of the layout of the sensor on a breadboard can be seen in Figure 7-1.

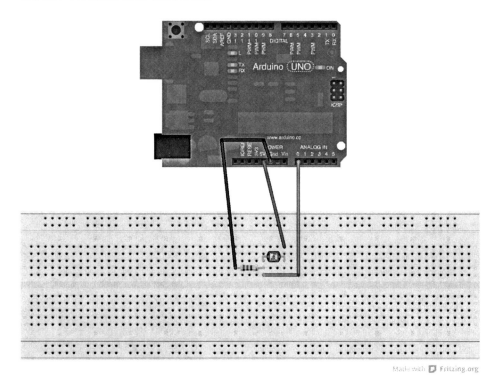

Figure 7-1. The photo sensor and 10K Ohm resistor connect to the Arduino

Now that you have a working photocell circuit, you want to make something happen that you can see. You will use the Adafruit motor shield again to use a stepper motor to turn when the photocell is above a certain threshold.

A stepper motor is a brushless DC motor that breaks its rotation into a defined number of steps around its 360 degree turn. Unlike the servo motor in previous projects, the motor can turn all the way around and continue turning without resetting. The stepper you are using is a unipolar stepper motor, so it has windings on two sides, and there are two sets of pairs of cables that need to be connected, plus a fifth wire to ground it. The stepper motor connected to the motor shield, in addition to the soldered photocell, can be seen in Figure 7-2.

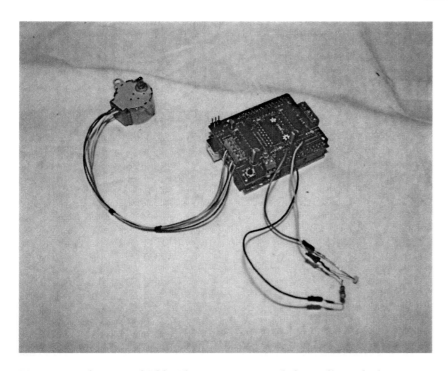

Figure 7-2. *The motor shield with stepper motor and photocell attached*

Programming the Box

Using the AFMotor library to control the stepper motor makes it a fairly simple process to code and utilize. The code for the box is shown in Listing 7-1.

Listing 7-1. The Light Controlled Motor

```
#include <AFMotor.h>

// Connect a stepper motor with 48 steps per revolution (7.5 degree)
// to motor port #1 (M1 and M2)
AF_Stepper motor(48, 1);

int photocellPin = A0;      // the cell and 10K pulldown are connected to a0
int photocellReading;       // the analog reading from the sensor divider
int threshold = 200;        // the amount of light required to activate the motor

void setup() {
  Serial.begin(9600);       // set up Serial library at 9600 bps

  motor.setSpeed(50);       // 50 rpm
}

void loop() {
    photocellReading = analogRead(photocellPin);
```

```
Serial.print("Photocell reading = ");
Serial.println(photocellReading);      // the raw analog reading

if (photocellReading > threshold) {
  motor.step(100, FORWARD, INTERLEAVE);
}


delay(100);
}
```

The first thing the code does is define the stepper motor for use. The code defines the motor as having 48 steps to make a single 360 degree rotation and using motor port one. On the motor shield, motor port one means it is using the M1 and M2 ports on the side of the motor shield, which are split by a ground port.

The photocell is an analog sensor, which runs from 0 to 1024 depending how much light is in the room. You define the photocell to be on Analog In pin 0, which is found on the side closer to the power plug (this is visible in Figure 1 as the pins closer to you).

The setup() function is used to define the speed of the motor. Since you are not utilizing a variable speed to the motor, you are defining the speed of the stepper motor in the motor in setup(). It's set for 50 revolutions per minute in the code, but you can consider other ways to adjust the speed later.

In the loop() function, you read in the value of the photocell and print it to the serial monitor to see how strong the light is. You check to see that the light is over 200, which is the threshold to take action.

A value of 200 should be high enough that the box needs to be open to start the motor once the photocell sees the light, but the number can be adjusted accordingly for different lighting situations.

The motor is told to step forward and will continue to do so with each execution of the loop while the photocell reading is above the threshold. If the motor is not triggered by the light or is triggered too easily, then adjust the threshold number.

Building the Box

Now you need to build the box. It will be narrow but tall. To build a more useful box, the dimensions can be adjusted accordingly. Start by building out the base with three layers of plates (see Figure 7-3).

Figure 7-3. *A stack of three plates creating a secure base*

With the base created, it's time to move the Arduino in and build the first layer of the walls to hold it in place.

Adding the Arduino

The motor and photocell will be going above the Arduino and motor shield when you are done, so put them to the sides while you build the walls, as shown in Figure 7-3.

Figure 7-4. *The Arduino is placed on the base and the first layer of bricks make up the walls*

The second layer of bricks is laid down on top of the first, as shown in Figure 7-5, with the wires still laid out around it.

Figure 7-5. *The second layer of bricks is added*

The third layer clears the USB and power ports. 1 x 4 bricks lead from the sides to the two 1 x 2 bricks stacked between the two ports, and the walls begin to circle the entire Arduino now, as shown in Figure 7-6.

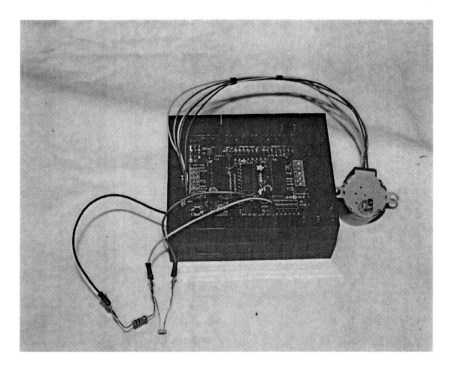

Figure 7-6. *The wall now covers over the ports as well, so the bricks surround the entire Arduino*

One more level of bricks is needed in order for the motor to have clearance to hang down from above the motor without making contact with the shield (see Figure 7-7).

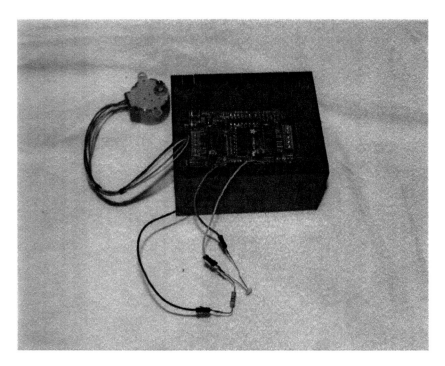

Figure 7-7. *The final level of wall bricks is laid down*

Adding the Motor

Since the motor is moving, there are vibrations, and it's a bad idea to have a motor in a metal casing rubbing against sensitive electronic parts. Start to turn bricks inward to give the visible part of the box a bottom with which to display your moving part. The layer of bricks will enclose the motor just enough for it to be able to hang from the motor. You will successively close the hole in as you add plates above it. A hole is also left for the photocell, as shown in Figure 7-8.

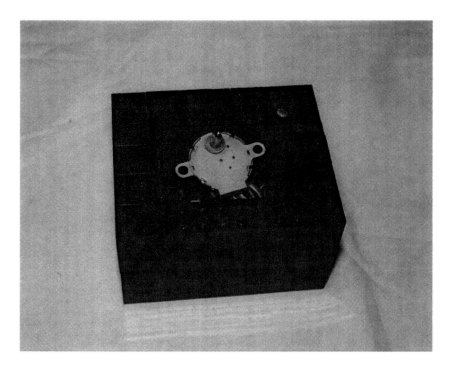

Figure 7-8. *Bricks are turned inwards to support the motor*

The bricks turned inwards are not very secure, so you should cover them with a layer of plates (see Figure 7-9). You won't be able to fully cover the motor yet, but enough of it can be covered to secure it in place, as well as lock the bricks in place. If the motor is still slightly higher than the level of the plates, then leave more of it uncovered and it will be taken care of in the following step.

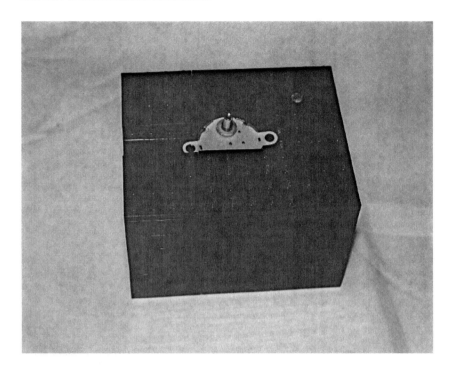

Figure 7-9. *A layer of plates is laid down to secure the bricks in place*

Figure 7-10 shows a second layer of plates laid down, this time covering everything but the shaft of the motor and the photocell. It's important to make sure that nothing is touching the shaft, since that will create friction as the shaft turns, wearing away the LEGO plate as well as affecting the performance of the motor.

Figure 7-10. *Another layer of plates coveres everything but the photocell and the motor shaft*

Adjusting the Wall Height

You need to know how tall the walls on top should be in order to cover whatever will turn on the shaft. In this example, you will have a fairy figure turning on the shaft and she is six bricks high. The first layer of the walls is laid out around her as you gauge her height and width for the box (see Figure 7-11).

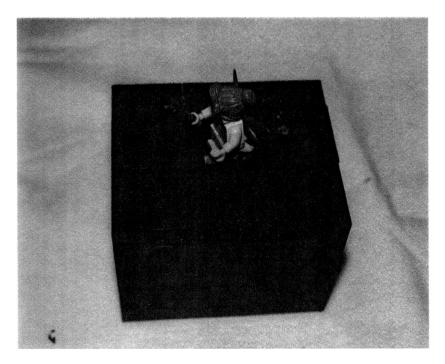

Figure 7-11. *The fairy is placed on top of the motor shaft and the walls are defined*

Now that you know what height the walls should be, you're going to build them up. Since you know the height needs to be six bricks high, you're going to build them that high. This height may vary based on what is placed on the shaft. You are also going to give it a staircase pattern by receding the edge one stud with each level added (see Figure 7-12).

Figure 7-12. *The walls are built high enough to encompass the minifigure on the shaft*

Adding Hinges

In order to be able to open and close the box, you need to add hinges. A layer of plates is added on top of the top layer of bricks, then a second layer is added with two click hinges placed with a stud between the hinge and the wall. The first two layers of plates can be seen in Figure 7-13 and the third layer, securing the hinges, can be seen in Figure 7-14.

Figure 7-13. *Two layers of plates are laid down, the second with click hinges*

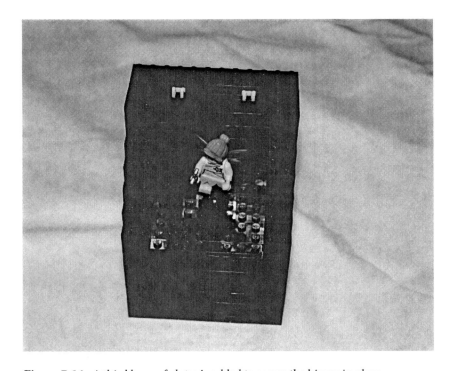

Figure 7-14. *A third layer of plates is added to secure the hinges in place*

Adding a Lid

Now that the hinges are done, you need a lid. It needs to be able to cover the exposed area of the opening of the box, so in this case it needs to be six bricks high. Note that it has a staircase pattern, complementary to the one you created on the wall, which can be seen in Figure 7-15.

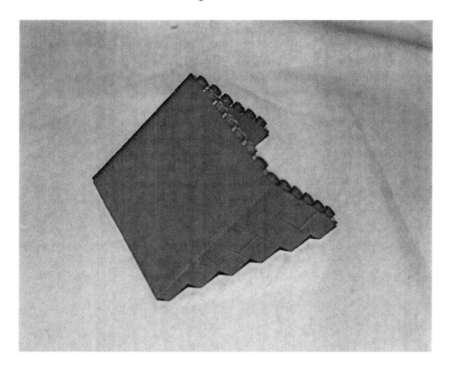

Figure 7-15. *The front and side of the lid*

The top of the lid needs to be able to hold the other half of the click hinges, so add some plates. The top of the lid will be three layer of plates again, but with the click hinges placed on the inside in positions that match the positions of the ones that have been put on top of the box. The lid with click places can be seen in Figure 7-16.

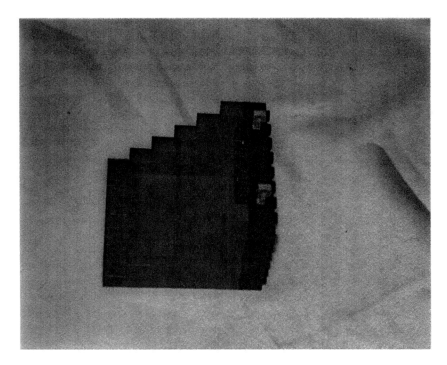

Figure 7-16. *The top of the lid of the box is three layers of plates with click hinges protruding*

Now you just need to attach the lid. The click hinges will snap into place and be able to freely open and close. It will also be able to hold the lid in place in several positions: fully open and closed, plus a few positions in between. Figure 7-17 shows the box with the lid installed and Figure 7-18 shows the completed box with the lid closed.

Figure 7-17. *The lid is snapped into place, completing the box*

Figure 7-18. *The lid comes down to hide its contents and block light to stop the figure from moving*

Summary

You just built the basis for a jewelry box or some other container that could have moving parts inside. Being able to read the climate outside, like current light or sound, gives you the ability to affect the world around you in different ways, not just triggering motors.

What else could you have the box do? Could it make noise or play music when it opens? Could it trigger some other projects or other devices when it opens? What could you hide in a box like this and protect by using the Arduino as a security device?

Parts List

The following is a list of parts needed to build the projects in each of the chapters. Images of all the parts can be found in the corresponding chapters. Each of the parts can easily be found online on web sites like SparkFun for electronic parts and BrickLink.com for LEGO parts.

Chapter 1: LEGO, Arduino, and the Ultimate Machine

Electronics

    1 Arduino Uno
    1 Adafruit Industries Motor Shield
    1 standard servo, TowerPro SG-5010
    1 toggle on/off switch

LEGO

    29 black 4 x 10 plates
    5 black 2 x 10 plates
    4 black 2 x 4 plates
    2 black 1 x 2 plates
    2 black 1 x 1 plates
    5 black 1 x 4 plates
    3 black 2 x 2 plates
    3 black 4 x 6 plates
    3 black 4 x 4 plates
    2 black 2 x 12 plates
    2 black 1 x 12 plates
    17 blue 2 x 2 bricks
    262 blue 1 x 2 bricks
    2 blue 1 x 1 bricks
    1 blue 2 x 4 brick
    2 blue 1 x 2 Technic bricks with a hole
    1 white 1 x 2 Technic brick with holes
    1 dark gray Technic liftarm 1 x 9
    2 dark gray Technic liftarms 2 x 4 L-shape
    1 5M light gray axle
    2 black Technic axle and pin connectors

3 black 1M Technic pins
4 light gray Technic axle connectors
10 11M Technic beams
18 black Technic pins
2 light gray Technic pins

Chapter 2: Using Sensors with the Android
Electronics

1 Arduino Uno
3 PING))) Ultrasonic Distance Sensor by Parallax, Inc.
22 gauge wire
3 LEDs

LEGO

620 green 1 x 2 bricks
93 green 2 x 4 bricks
23 green 1 x 1 bricks
24 green 2 x 2 bricks
23 green 1 x 4 bricks
4 blue Techic 1 x 2 bricks
22 white 1 x 2 bricks
5 white 2 x 4 bricks
2 white 2 x 3 bricks
6 white 1 x 1 bricks
26 white 1 x 2 tiles
6 white 2 x 2 tiles
1 blue round 2 x 2 brick
1 light gray Technic 2 x 4 plate with holes
1 light gray 5M Technic axle
1 light gray Technic wedge-belt wheel
2 black Technic pins
2 green minifigure legs

Chapter 3: Twitter Pet
Electronics

1 Arduino Uno
1 Arduino Ethernet Shield
2 ultra bright red LEDs
22 gauge wire

LEGO

29 black 4 x 10 plates
2 black 2 x 10 plates
2 black 4 x 4 plates
30 black 1 x 2 plates
2 black 4 x 8 plates
49 black 2 x 4 bricks
9 black 1 x 2 bricks
4 black 2 x 2 bricks
4 black 1 x 1 bricks
2 black 1 x 4 bricks
1 black 1 x 1 round plate
203 white 1 x 2 bricks
20 white 1 x 1 bricks
40 white 2 x 4 bricks
16 white 2 x 2 bricks
3 white Technic 1 x 2 bricks with holes
1 dark gray 3M Technic beam
2 white 7M Technic beams
2 black Technic pins

Chapter 4: RFID and the Crystal Ball

Electronics

1 Arduino Uno
2 SparkFun glass capsule RFID tags
1 SparkFun ID-12 RFID reader
1 SparkFun ID-12 RFID reader breakout board
6 ultra bright red LEDs

LEGO

24 black 4 x 10 plates
2 black 4 x 8 plates
2 black 2 x 10 plates
4 black 4 x 4 plates
4 black 1 x 10 plates
33 black 2 x 4 bricks
10 black 1 x 2 bricks
3 black 2 x 2 bricks
4 black 2 x 3 bricks
2 black 1 x 1 bricks
2 red 2 x 2 bricks
1 red 2 x 4 brick
104 translucent blue 1 x 2 bricks
142 translucent blue 2 x 2 bricks
24 translucent blue 1 x 1 bricks

11 black round 2 x 2 bricks
16 white round 2 x 2 bricks
1 black round 2 x 2 tile
1 32 M Technic pin

Chapter 5: Animating the TARDIS

Electronics

1 Arduino Uno
1 Adafruit Industries Wav Shield
1 speaker

LEGO

8 blue 1 x 10 plates
1 blue 1 x 1 plate
101 blue 1 x 2 plates
32 blue 1 x 6 plates
13 blue 2 x 2 plates
5 blue 2 x 4 plates
42 blue 2 x 8 plates
25 blue 4 x 4 plates
192 blue 1 x 2 jumper plates
1 blue 2 x 4 Technic plate
52 blue 1 x 1 bricks
223 blue 1 x 2 bricks
1 blue 1 x 4 brick
98 blue 1 x 6 bricks
112 blue 2 x 2 bricks
2 blue 2 x 4 bricks
6 blue 2 x 6 bricks
73 blue 2 x 8 bricks
18 blue 1 x 2 tiles
4 blue 1 x 6 tiles
8 blue 1 x 4 tiles
84 blue 1 x 8 tiles
1 blue 2 x 2 rounded tile
4 sets of blue hinges
23 blue modified 2 x 2 bricks
8 white 1 x 1 bricks
40 white 1 x 2 bricks
8 white 1 x 1 Technic bricks
24 blue ½ Technic pins
14 blue 1 x 2 Technic bricks
36 blue 45 degree slopes
12 blue 45 degree corner slopes
2 trans clear 2 x 2 rounds
4 blue 1 x 2 – 1 x 4 brackets

Chapter 6: Controlling LEGO Trains With Arduino

Electronics

1 Arduino Uno
7 ultra bright red LEDs
1 infrared LED
1 normal open push button
1 potentiometer
1 220 Ohm resistor

LEGO for Train Station

1 black 1 x 1 plate
14 black 1 x 2 plates
1 black 1 x 3 plate
11 black 1 x 4 plates
1 black 2 x 2 plate
1 black 2 x 6 plate
1 black 2 x 8 plate
3 black 2 x 10 plates
3 black 4 x 4 plates
27 black 4 x 10 plates
24 white 1 x 2 bricks
8 white 2 x 4 bricks
7 white 1 x 2 Technic bricks
Decorative LEGO pieces including chairs, minifigures, clocks, etc.

LEGO for Train

Train base
Train motor
Train wheels
Train battery pack
16 red 1 x 1 bricks
71 red 1 x 2 bricks
15 red 2 x 4 bricks
4 red 33 3 x 1 slopes
2 red 33 3 x 4 slopes
3 blue 2 x 2 rounded bricks
2 black 6 x 6 plates
1 conductor minifigure

Chapter 7: Building a Light Sensitive Box

Electronics

1 Arduino Uno
1 Adafruit Industries Motor Shield
1 10k protocell
1 10k resistor
1 stepper motor

LEGO

8 black 4 x 10 plates
3 black 2 x 12 plates
42 black 1 x 2 plates
24 black 2 x 2 plates
4 black 2 x 4 plates
7 black 4 x 4 plates
1 black 4 x 6 plate
4 black 1 x 1 plates
14 black 1 x 2 plates
2 black 6 x 8 plates
1 black 1 x 3 plate
4 black 1 x 4 plates
6 black 1 x 1 bricks
26 black 1 x 2 bricks
2 black x`1 x 3 bricks
2 black 1 x 4 bricks
2 black 1 x 10 bricks
21 black 2 x 3 bricks
3 black 2 x 2 bricks
32 black 2 x 4 bricks
39 red 1 x 2 bricks
1 red 1 x 8 brick
2 light gray hinge plates 1 x 2 with 2 fingers on end
2 light gray hinge plates 1 x 2 with 1 finger on end

Index

■ U, V, W, X, Y, Z

CPSIA information can be obtained at www.ICGtesting.com
Printed in the USA
LVOW112009170613

338961LV00012B/443/P